Free
Your
Voice

Free Your Voice

Awaken to Life Through Singing

Silvia Nakkach
and Valerie Carpenter

SOUNDS TRUE
BOULDER, COLORADO

Sounds True, Inc.
Boulder, CO 80306

Published 2012

Cover by Shara Gardner

Book design by Rachael Murray

Illustrations © Shara Gardner

Printed in the United States of America

Library of Congress Cataloging-in-Publication Data

Nakkach, Silvia.

Free your voice : awaken to life through singing / by Silvia Nakkach and Valerie Carpenter.

    pages cm

Includes bibliographical references.

ISBN 978-1-60407-800-8 — ISBN 978-1-60407-833-6

    1. Singing—Instruction and study. 2. Music--Physiological aspects. 3. Music—Psychological aspects. 4. Yoga. I. Carpenter, Valerie. II. Title.

MT820.N296 2012

783—dc23

    2012002370

Enhanced ebook ISBN: 978-1-60407-841-1

10 9 8 7 6 5 4 3 2

To my music teacher Ali Akbar Khan (Khansahib)
To my mind teacher Chögyal Namkhai Norbu
To my cosmic father Pai Dary
May your love and light shine through these pages

In memory of Michael Ross Knapp and Dr. Clive Robbins

"Music is like food. When you need it you don't have to explain why, because it is basic to life."
ALI AKBAR KHAN

Contents

Guided Audio Practices

Throughout the book, you will find guided audio practices that will help deepen your experience. Visit SoundsTrue.com/ FreeYourVoice to download these practices.

Foreword

As an oncologist, I use sound and music therapy as part of my medical practice on a regular basis. For my patients, seeing a cancer specialist for the first time is one of the most stressful experiences of their lives. In new-patient consultations at Gaynor Integrative Oncology, traditional modalities such as chemotherapy, radiation, and surgery are reviewed along with blood tests, scans, and nutritional factors. I then offer patients the music therapy described in my book, *The Healing Power of Sound*. After a session, invariably patients tell me that they feel more relaxed and peaceful than they have ever felt before. In this way, on the most stressful day of a patient's life, he or she can also experience the greatest peace as well. How is this possible? The answer is combining sound, music, and chanting with a path of true self-discovery.

I have for years played Silvia Nakkach's music and chanting CDs over the office sound system for the benefit of my patients. I find her book *Free Your Voice* to be a delightful and enthralling read. It makes a significant contribution toward revitalizing the ancient paradigm of singing as a healing practice or yoga. Drawing on her vast and extraordinarily diverse musical experience, Silvia presents the individual's singing voice as an instrument of universal music, beyond any cultural divide and transcending notions of personal skill. She integrates a range of different cultures into one coherent and fresh musical reality.

Singing is a divine gift. Silvia emphasizes that singing is a birthright for us all—not just those people we call "singers." In fact, the most transformative kind of singing happens when we are not singing like singers, but offering song, chant, or sound as medicine and devotion. Everybody is invited to sing and join the universal choir: scientists, artists, healers, and teachers.

Reading this book is a joyful reminder that we are all born with a potent musical instrument: the voice. It has an organic impulse to explore and express, to refine and offer, to transcend and heal. The voice has the power to connect the body, the inner self, and the outer world. The voice can express words of power, and it has a unique potential to make music, relax the body, connect with inner peace, clear the mind—all while activating the pre-frontal part of the brain through its natural overtones and versatility.

Free Your Voice traces the power of the singing voice back to its most ancient roots as a devotional art and demonstrates its future as an integrative medicine that promotes relaxation and lessens fear and pain. It provides a deeper understanding of the musical form and structure that informs the voice, offering at the same time a therapeutic and spiritual experience. Each section of the book and the accompanying audio tracks illustrate how skillfully Silvia has assimilated the ancient wisdom teachings of sound, three decades of classical Indian singing, and a lifelong immersion in contemporary vocal improvisation. She has woven these threads of experience into an offering that is as enriching to the general reader as to the professional musician or the experienced healer.

We can now experience singing the same way that Silvia experiences her voice, as a liberating and liquid beauty. We have been invited to gather our voices in an affirmative connection to life and the joy of it. I foresee many readers coming back to these pages to re-read Silvia's message, reaching as far into the future as this book reaches into the ancient wisdom of the past.

Mitchell L. Gaynor, MD

President of Gaynor Integrative Oncology

Assistant Professor of Medicine at Weill-Cornell Medical College

Author of *The Healing Power of Sound: Recovery from Life-Threatening Illness Using Sound, Voice, and Music*

Preface by Valerie Carpenter

In the summer of 2007, a series of personal investigations led me to The Voice Loft in Emeryville, California, where I was granted my first taste of the phenomenon that is Silvia Nakkach. In retrospect, I could say the Hand of Fate plopped me down at the feet of a master, one who continues to guide the opening of my voice, my heart, my imagination, and my spirit in ways I could not have fathomed a year earlier.

It was a Thursday Night Chanting Group. About a dozen individuals—all, I was convinced, consummate singers a hair's breadth away from a career at the Met—sat on cushions on a well-worn Persian rug, adjusting portable recording devices, stretching their supple limbs, and sipping tea. I felt I had stumbled upon a coterie of accomplished vocal artists and free-spirited spiritual adepts.

As I adjusted my own limbs in what I hoped was a good approximation of a seasoned yogi, Silvia took her place in the circle. Framed by a mane of honey-colored hair, she sat down on a makeshift throne of raised cushions draped in velvet, and faced an intriguing box-like instrument I later learned was called a harmonium. She adjusted the position of an impressive-looking microphone (into which she made those mysterious cooing sounds musicians make when they are coaxing their electronic brethren to interact with us mere mortals), and cleared her throat several times.

After instructing us to take a few long, slow breaths, moving our "hands as clouds," and to adjust our *boondas* (short for *abondanzas,* or buttocks, as they say in Brazil), she began to sing.

As everyone in the room had their eyes closed, I knowingly closed mine as well and . . . oh! Suddenly I was in a mystical forest and before me appeared an Angel whose soft, splendid, limpid voice beckoned me to follow deeper and deeper into the trees. The Angel would sing a few notes and I had no choice but to sing them back. And although there were only two of us in that magical forest, whenever I sang my ardent reply a chorus of voices joined mine in a communal longing to come closer, to delve deeper, to become one with the sweet promise of that angelic voice.

Let me make it perfectly clear that at that point in my life, I did not sing. I would say, "could not sing," but I have since learned from Silvia that those words are "illegal" language, and she would not permit me to say them in this preface. Nevertheless, despite a thirty-year career as a professional actress, at that time, for many reasons I could unproudly defend, I simply did not sing.

But that night, as the trodden red Persian rug transformed into a magical flying carpet and that Angel seduced my voice into pursuing her into ever more sublime realms, the Singer in me awakened.

Now, I don't expect to be making appearances any time soon on the stage of the Metropolitan Opera or *American Idol,* but I discovered in Silvia's Yoga of the Voice program a really enjoyable method for learning how to sing. In addition, I found a deeply satisfying spiritual practice through singing—a musical path to bliss.

I have since learned that the approach Silvia was using on that July night is an ancient practice known as call-and-response and that the exotic syllables we were singing back to her came from Sanskrit and various indigenous languages. The people in the room—some with musical backgrounds, others with none—came from all walks of life but shared the yearning to dwell in that sacred inner realm where Silvia and her magic voice so skillfully led us.

Over the past five years that I have had the great privilege of studying with Silvia, I have seen people of all ages, cultures, and backgrounds flock to her classes and workshops. On one occasion, as I watched her fly across a room filled with a hundred people, I saw her virtually transform into a rare exotic bird with extravagant plumage, both ageless and achingly young. She was so full of joy as the participants, mostly city clerks and firefighters, danced after her chanting a Sanskrit verse to a bossa nova beat.

In Silvia's artistry, you will encounter a unique blend of the ancient and the modern, the contemplative and the expressive, the East and the West. Raised in several countries as the daughter of a diplomat, I have heard her say that she is the only person she knows who speaks five different languages—each with an accent foreign to the land in which she learned it.

When we first spoke about writing this book together, I was a bit taken aback by my own presumption. After all, as well as being a consummate musician, Silvia is also an impressive scholar and trained psychologist who has expertly written articles in publications around the globe. We soon discovered, however, that the teaching voice, which flows so naturally and exuberantly as Silvia works with groups of all kinds, is different from the voice of the academic. It is the voice of the dynamic teacher, the gentle guide, and the powerful master that we hope to capture in this book.

It became my job to be the conduit for the voice of the teacher to reach the ears of you, the reader. It is a challenge at times to simultaneously contain and convey the vitality and abundance that characterizes Silvia's expression and so profoundly inspires her students. Her ideas often spiral into great galaxies of inspiration and imagination that ultimately synthesize into a meaningful whole. And how can the written word transmit the resonance of the rich pan-global accent that rings in my ears as I am writing? Then there is her humor, which always seems to stem from the joy bubbling up inside her, until it spills into her down-to-earth pragmatism and love for simple things like shopping. So when you find yourself soaring on a sentence rich with metaphors and sublime inspiration only to find yourself plopped down with a grin squarely on your boondas, that is all Silvia.

I humbly offer this effort in the hopes that your journey with the Yoga of the Voice will yield as many bountiful rewards for you as they have for me. And try to see Silvia in person when you can. It's an experience of a lifetime.

Silvia, my most sincere thanks to you for helping me to reveal my authentic voice . . . as I hope to faithfully render yours into words that will reach the hearts of the readers of these pages.

Valerie Carpenter

Introduction

After working for countless years with an approach to the voice that is as innovative as it is ancient—an approach cultivated from direct experience; from the heart; from the birds in the sky; from my deep background in classical music; from my teachers who gave me the best training in the world; from the South, North, East, and West—I am so happy to share this experience with you, dear reader, in these pages.

This is not a book about "how to sing"—although if you choose to follow the path, your voice will naturally open in beauty, power, and freedom of expression. This book is a guide for discovering the potential of your own voice to unlock and cultivate creative and spiritual energy. It's about building the bank account that will preserve the most precious capital you have: your emotional well-being.

I call the systematic approach to this discovery The Yoga of the Voice. Yoga is an integrative path toward our experience of liberation and bliss—just as yogic practices of breathing, meditation, or body postures (called *asanas* in Sanskrit) can bring freedom from a mundane, ego-centered state to an experience of divine inspired energy. A patient, disciplined practice of releasing your voice can lead you to a higher spiritual dimension where creativity, connectedness, and communion abound.

Singing is a joyful, natural activity. Making music can be like flying—a liberating practice that frees us from conditioning, from ego, from karmic traces, from anything that tightens us up. So many people have the false idea that before they can engage in this joyful birthright, they need to learn how to read music or have musical training or be a "real" singer. When we listen to and do practices from the ancient cultures—the indigenous and shamanic cultures—we begin to understand that this idea is nonsense, a form of "musical materialism" in our culture that tells us we must consume more information, more training, more books, more CDs and gadgets before we are free to use our own natural voice.

It is much easier than that. The most important piece is to commit to the path of personal devotion—and then to sing. I intend to demystify the process of singing for you, as I have done for my students (some of them "trained" singers, others with little or no musical background, and many in between) for more than thirty years. From this demystification, I intend to lead you to engage with the subtle qualities of the voice, the true mysticism of music, breath, and sound.

These ideas are very ancient. If we go back to the origin of the word "singing," it means to make an incantation, to enchant, to make magic. Making magic means inviting fantasy. When you become familiar with fantasy, with the way you use your imagination and intuition to engage higher states of being (where the materialistic realities do not lead), you are truly learning to sing. You are tuned to your own Discovery Channel . . . *it's fantastic.*

We all have the capacity to connect with energy that liberates us and with energy that constrains us. We are made of vibration, and we have an unconditional potential inside of us to resonate with all kinds of vibrational fields. We are all born as pure beings, pure beauty. We just have to reconnect and reawaken that purity, that space of no limitations where boundaries dissolve and spiritual freedom flourishes.

My way is through the voice, and the path is carefully designed with yoga-based practices that integrate subtle movements of breath, tone, music, and mind. I tell my students that the best way to free their voices from their bodies is to give them as an offering. In that spirit, I offer you this book. May it assist you in realizing your dreams of bliss and ecstatic union.

Silvia Nakkach

Invocation

In a bowl filled with sacred frequencies
Precious chants dance

Energy moves slowly boundlessly
The spirit finds dwelling
Abiding in sacred inwardness
Fearlessly
Embracing
The nature of music
As sound in time

Easy vitality
Greets the devotional pace of peace
Emotions flow
Through holy rivers of rasa
Sheltered by sweet nectar of lineage
Spirit becomes experience

The practice is the answer
Confident daily effort
The stairway to delight
Repetition

The groove of the universe
The joyful energy of the voice
Awakens the sun
Inside
Chanting the names

We resonate with nature
We believe that we believe
Urge for results fades
In the infinite radiance of the journey

The open heart surrenders to the path
Through the indestructible fire of mantra
The same mantra
Everyday
A bit longer
A bit more complex in its simplicity
In the continual magic of duration
When time becomes space
Resting on the throne of the singing drone
Playing the mandala of our dancing finger-tips
I remember
You remember
We remember
Our freedom

And in reverence
We bow
Who is singing?
Who is singing?

Sacredness melts in sound
Sound dissolves into silence

It is not duty but beauty
It is not duty but beauty
It is not duty but beauty

The transcendent mantra
Is heard
Everywhere . . .

Come, come, come . . .
Sing, sing, sing . . .

Everyone is welcome!
We all can share
This planet called "Music"

And remember . . .
Remember to forget
That you are singing

Silvia Nakkach

1

Learning from the Birds

Birdsong brings relief
to my longing.
RUMI, translated by Coleman Barks

The singing voice is a vehicle connecting us with the flow of life that gushes through our being at full force. The singing voice, through the media of breath and sound, supports the process of transforming energy patterns, creates measurable beneficial effects in the physical body, and influences consciousness more efficiently than any other form of sound. Like no other sound, the voice becomes a link with our spiritual life by revealing deeper aspects of the Self.

My primary intention in writing this book is to remind us that we are born wanting to sing and that at any stage of life we can benefit from singing more. Singing starts in the womb and continues blissfully throughout our lives— on the playground, at the ballpark, at political rallies, in the concert hall, in our morning worship. Unsolicited singing emerges as an organic impulse to express out loud our membership in the universal community choir. We love it, and we long for more.

This book is based on the absolute belief that *everybody* can sing. In these pages, you will find a systematic method for freeing the voice to promote physical health and emotional well-being, encourage self-expression, cultivate artistry, and nurture happiness.

The media is buzzing lately with "new" discoveries of how sound, vibration, and music can benefit our health and well-being. These benefits, now recognized by science, have been intuitively known by the human species throughout history. We can learn about this from the ancients, as well as from many indigenous people living today. The fact is that each and every one of us carries with us, at all times, a most valuable instrument for healing: our own natural voice.

When you start opening your voice—whether in a hum, through sounding long tones, by improvising, or with a favorite song—it's like a fountain and you can't stop the flow. If you keep yourself "in the open" by vocalizing every day (or as often as you can), your voice becomes your protection, your Buddha mind, your fountain of wealth and health, a soothing balm, the precious child that you adore, your chosen mother.

With regular practice, vocalizing, singing, and chanting become an ordinary miracle that effortlessly guides you to a sense of self-confidence, compassion, and love supreme. Your savings account toward radiant health and spiritual liberation will grow fat and happy!

My Secret Religion

Since my early childhood, birds and their natural songs have inspired me. When I was small, I talked to the birds and they talked back to me. They became my secret religion. I would sit on the stairs of our weekend home and listen to their songs for hours.

When I was five years old, nature was my sanctuary, and the mystery of listening became the gateway to my deepest inner world. My top-secret sonic meditation was to earnestly attend to the space of time between one song and the next from the same bird. It thrilled me to discover that the space in between was not always the same—what in music we refer to as periodic rhythmic pulse. The birdsongs were so beautiful, and it was captivating for me to discover this "space in between." The appreciation that nature is not linear was the awakening of musicality within my five-year-old self. The cycles of the creative imagination seem to have the same nonlinear, poetic nature.

Another fun sonic game was to imagine what the bird was saying and to create fantastical stories based on the call and response among birds. But my favorite listening experience led me to discover the freedom of my voice and its connection with my own wild nature. I would echo the songbird with my voice and engage in a nuanced dialogue that would continue the next day, and the next. I adored this story singing—my first experience of sacredness in music—and I still play this listening game with the same wonderment and devotion.

The birds made me so happy I wanted to learn how I could use their special magic to make other people happy. As a singer, I wondered how I could soar to such heights with my own voice. As a voice teacher, I wondered how I could assist others in allowing their voices to fly. My fascination took me to many world paradises in search of particular bird songs. For many years I researched the human voice, determined to explore every aspect of sound it can utter.

Who Is Singing?

> *Keep on knocking, and the joy inside*
> *will eventually open a window*
> *and look out to see who's there.*
> RUMI, translated by Coleman Barks

I noticed that singing in a slow, sustained, and sliding manner induces a profound shift in emotions and states of consciousness. In the system of practices that I designed, the voice wanders through a combination of long tones, trancelike repetitive patterns, devotional chants, indigenous songs, invocations, and textural poetry.

Through working with the voice in this way, the realm of sounding becomes a state of consciousness—a kind of trance— where the attention is not on the Self, but in the experience of Sound. Free from selfish demands, the voice soars and releases divine tones and songs. We wonder, *Who is singing?*

Many times I hear my students ask, "Who was that? . . . Was that *me?*" I tell them, "Yes, it was! You were just listening, focused only on sound, and your voice responded with confident freedom."

The practice of *being* in sound, *dwelling* in sound, becomes a devotional gift. We begin to realize that we are not singing, but calling in divine qualities; we are not performing but *transforming*—simultaneously playing and praying. Here there is no singer, only breath, attention, and tone.

In this meditation-like state, singing becomes a doorway to deep inner silence, where we are one with pure vibration. The heart is open, the voice is open, the hands are open, the eyes are softly closed—we experience no fear. Our breath is the breath of God.

Singing in this way clears the mind of everything else but sound—instantly. Abiding in the true nature of the mind— empty and clear as crystal—we soon experience the energizing power of the voice.

Freedom settles and we allow for more and more of this irresistible joy—the joy I first heard in the music of the birds. We open ourselves to the mystery of *whoever is singing!*

THE YOGA OF THE VOICE

*Music is yoga, a way to reach God; through
music you can give more love to this world.*
ALI AKBAR KHAN

I was quite young in the late sixties when I discovered yoga. My
teacher was an unusual combination of Germanic austerity and
Hindu holy man. We were doing many classes and weeklong
retreats that included body postures, fasting, various cleansing practices, meditation, and, of course, chanting. Everything
about that practice and that community lingers in my memory
as *perfect*—enjoyable and healthy to the utmost.

It was in those glorious days that the seed for my Yoga of the
Voice program was planted. I have been cultivating this garden
ever since, traveling almost every year to India and teaching
thousands of students around the world to enter transpersonal
realms through a nondual approach to singing. The Vox Mundi
School of the Voice—with centers in California, Brazil, India,
and Argentina (see the resources section for more information)—is dedicated to teaching this approach to singing, as well
as to performing and preserving ancient and unusual vocal arts.
This book represents the unfolding of a lifelong pursuit as I
share with you the technique, philosophy, science, and magic
that infuse the practice.

I have studied many different kinds of yoga since those early
days, and I began to realize that yoga is really a state of mind
that stimulates us to become one with "good" things, while
protecting us from "bad" things. Illuminating the connection
between yoga, "goodness," and the voice became my quest.

The word *yoga* means "to put together." So what is it we are
trying to put together? When I asked this question at a recent
Yoga of the Voice workshop, the students had some very nice
poetic answers like "sound and silence," "yin and yang," and
"earth and sky."

While all these impressions are valid, what we are actually doing is putting together a curriculum—a series of practices designed to liberate the conditions of the mind into a state of spiritual insight and bliss. The disciplined practice of music as yoga is one of the most powerful ways to embody the sacred and mystic texture of reality—and the voice is the most energetic agent to facilitate this transmission of power.

The use of sound and vibration in yoga is as old as yoga itself. The Yoga of the Voice integrates many traditions of sonorous yogic practices, including sacred sound formulas, mantras, and chants to burn away impurities of the body and the mind; clear emotions; and, ultimately, to attain liberation from all conditions.

We enhance our repertoire with chants and songs from indigenous cultures around the world—such as the Yoruba in Africa (re-energized through Afro-Brazilian music), India, and the shamanic traditions of Tibet, Europe, and the Americas—all of which have sacred sound in common as a vehicle to access higher and subtler states of consciousness, inner transformation, and healing.

I've woven these practices together to free the voice and clear the mind and heart through singing and sounding. The method includes and goes beyond classic Western vocal technique by integrating it with the spirited discipline of yoga.

As a footnote, I like to use *yoga* as a verb: with attention, diligence, and dedication, we can yoga our mind, body, and voice into bliss. Through this yogic approach to singing, the sacred ceases to be something external to us, and we infuse our practice with a higher sense of appreciation that is devotionally intoxicating.

How to Use This Book

The book is a series of connected short teachings, healing practices, and musical explorations that use the voice as the primary instrument for making music and keeping you healthy. In these pages, along with the downloadable audios, we will guide you to develop and deepen your Yoga of the Voice practice. We embark on a journey where the destinations include:

How to develop a practice of breath and voice, performed with consistency and imagination, where sound designs its own landscapes through the expressive power of the voice

A series of sonorous yogic practices that involve subtle movements and the sustained focus of the mind in sound

A gentle path for developing a voice that is fully embodied, uniquely expressive, and played like a fine musical instrument

Invocatory words and ancient seed sounds that deliver explicit spiritual information for expansion of consciousness and well-being

A beginning repertory of mantras and chants from many cultures that you can build on and share as you deepen your practice

Techniques for vocal improvisation to engage your singing imagination and enrich your musical offerings

How to foster confidence and kindness toward yourself as a vulnerable chanteur of the universal song

How to cultivate singing as a spiritual practice for yourself and to serve a larger community

Each chapter represents a station on your journey toward effortless singing. Your job is to become familiar with each section—making of each practice a friend, creating your own vocal family of techniques, and, finally, assembling a repertoire of practices of your choosing.

Throughout the book, you will find exercises that you can use to design a personal Yoga of the Voice routine. In the context of yoga, it is helpful to expand our notion of practice from the physical dimension of "exercise" into the more holistic dimension of *asana,* which means posture or pose and comes from the Sanskrit root meaning "to be present." These asanas, which engage sound, body, and consciousness, will become your allies—those unconditional friends that make you feel relaxed and safe. When you come upon a practice, I invite you to read it through and then to put the book down and try it— like the following.

exercise 1 Open Sound / Any Sound

This practice opens the voice, releases tension and fatigue, relaxes tired muscles, restores energy, and refreshes the mind. It is especially good for clearing worry, distress, or tension that has accumulated during the day.

1. Stand comfortably with your weight balanced on both feet.

2. Tune in to your body and release the first sound that wants to come out. It may be a sigh, a soft groan, or even a vocal explosion of sound. Let whatever sound that wants to be expressed come without judgment.

3. Tune in again and let out another sound, and then another. Tune in and sound. You may find that with each sound you release, your body finds a new starting place and the expression of sound becomes more expansive and playful.

4. Allow your body and voice to interact in this way for as long as you like. When you are finished, stand quietly and notice how your body and your energy feel.

Try this practice with a group and you may find yourselves making a symphony of joyous release.

You may observe that every practice takes you on its own separate journey and that you end up in a different place from where you started. As you experience each one, take a silent rest, allowing yourself to become aware of the subtle changes in your state of being. You may choose to record your sonic adventures in a journal or with a recording device. Consider this practice your passport to exotic destinations.

I encourage you to read this book first from beginning to end. Then use it like a mantra, living each chapter and repeating each practice again and again. The circular power of the mantra will purify your mind and protect your voice from any unsupportive habits. A glossary at the end of the book will assist you with any unfamiliar terms.

The digital audio downloads that pair with this book have demonstrations and practices that will help you integrate the teachings. When you see the audio icon (▶), you can refer to that audio track for further instruction, a demonstration, or the chance to sing along. You can access this book's audios by visiting SoundsTrue.com/FreeYourVoice.

The audios are meant to provide you with the reassuring presence of the teacher. They guide you creatively through a Yoga of the Voice session that includes many of the exercises presented in the text. Several tracks are based on the ancient call-and-response technique. With these selections, you can sing seed sounds, mantras, chants, lullabies, and indigenous songs as you embark on guided musical journeys by singing your response to the call. Track 2, called "A Drone for Your

Practice," offers a ten-minute musical drone—a long-tone accompaniment based on the interval of a fifth, continuously sounded throughout—that you can use in your own practice whenever a drone is required.

While practicing with the audios, keep returning to the book— the text will deepen your capacity to integrate and embody the teachings. As you go back and forth between book, audios, and your personal practice, you may find that layers of musical insight and appreciation continue to unfold and enfold you.

The Yoga of the Voice is devoted to fostering confidence and personal autonomy when you sing. I wish for you to become an independently wealthy troubadour of the inspired word.

2

Music as Medicine
WHY IT'S GOOD TO SING EVERY DAY

You see more and more . . . why healing is
happening through music. It's because music
causes a reorganization of the tonal structure,
and Man in essence is a vibration. The
molecule sings, the heart of the atom is tone
. . . Man has a sound body (that has been
proven scientifically). The reason there is so
much illness is that he is not pitched in tune
with his Sound Body.
KENNETH G. MILLS, *From Tone to a Sound Principle*

Have you ever wondered what it would feel like to *sing*
yourself to health? Or to use singing as your daily meditation?
Or your spiritual practice? It might go something like this:

"When we were singing, I could feel and see the sun. Warmth
kept pouring all over me."

"It felt like a long dip in the ocean."

"Singing allows me to adjust myself deep within. On a cellular level, it feels like it brings into balance and harmony all that vibrates in my body and soul. It centers and grounds me like nothing I've ever done before."

"I can feel the vibrations penetrating every cell. It's like the cells are actually changing—at the same time expanding and letting go of anything that's not healthy."

"It's like my whole bio-psychological system is being recalibrated and renewed."

"I had a headache for three days, but after singing for an hour, it's gone—and my sinuses are clear, too!"

"I'm so calm . . . "

"I feel filled with joy . . . "

"Wow!"

These words are from students all over the world. I enjoy listening to their spontaneous responses after we've been singing together even for a few minutes. Usually they speak of feeling more relaxed, energetic, aligned, and spacious. Physically, headaches and bodily pains disappear, muscles relax, sinuses open. Students speak of the mind becoming clearer and more focused, of dark moods or depression lifting. Even more often they reveal deep feelings of connection and bliss—and sometimes surprising insights regarding their health. Over and over, I hear the voice of self-trust arising as the singing voice grows freer and a sense of possibility opens up for those who are facing physical or emotional challenges.

BORN TO SING

Why should the simple act of singing fill us with so much trust and joy? I believe it goes back to the fact that every adult was once a baby, comforted by the sound of a female voice. As a fetus, we were continuously serenaded by an uninterrupted symphony of sounds from our mother's belly, the flow of her blood, the beating of her heart. The sound of our mother's voice is in fact our earliest communication with the world beyond our fetal nest. In almost every culture, spontaneous lullabies emerge to satisfy a primary instinct in mothers to communicate with their babies. Perhaps we were lucky enough to have a mother who hummed or sang to us in the womb. In any case, the human voice, especially the singing voice, can have a deeply soothing effect that recalls the voice of the mother. This is our first and closest encounter with human resonance.

Thanks to the groundbreaking work of renowned twentieth-century French physician, Alfred Tomatis—considered by many to be the father of modern psychoacoustics—we now know that the ears of the fetus are fully developed by twenty weeks of age.[1] That means we are able to hear all the gushing, whooshing orchestra of life around us while we are cradled in our mother's womb. We become entrained to the rhythm of her heart and her footsteps. Studies reveal that infants will instantly calm down when they are played a recording that replicates the resting heartbeat of seventy-two beats per minute, while infants who are played a recording of 120 beats per minute will become visibly agitated.[2]

As the first sense organ to fully develop, the ears are the captain of our sensory team, possessing the neuroconnections necessary for the rest of our senses to function efficiently. The fetal ear is also the organ of primal bonding. Receiving sound, responding to sound, and ultimately producing sound is a fundamental primal instinct. We are programmed to be vibration-sensing sound beings.

It's a natural and healthy impulse for mothers to sing to their unborn babies. I continually get requests from pregnant women to help them communicate with their unborn babies through singing. In my many years of teaching and therapeutic work, I have seen numerous babies born into our singing community. These babies are very comfortable with sound and music. They are serious listeners, and they clearly respond to music dynamics, volume, and noise. Many of them, when they start growing up, beg to come to our chanting sessions; even as they play quietly in a corner or watch videos on little machines, they are delighted to share—again—the devotional listening landscape we create. We love these babies! I was one of them.

A MUSICAL PATH TO HEALTH

Our voice reminds us of our deepest bonding, and it also supports our whole body-mind connection. Research shows that singing and chanting used as a healing modality stimulates healthy brain cells, lowers blood pressure, promotes deep breathing, boosts the immune system, and regulates heart rhythm.[3] We experience these effects as greater relaxation, reduced stress, enhanced concentration and focus, and elevated mood. As an added benefit, the healing power of singing also takes us beyond habitual ego-boundaries to transcendent states of consciousness and uplifting experiences of wholeness.

Scientists are now studying these effects, although people throughout the ages have known intuitively about the health benefits of chanting and singing. Ancient Tibetan yogis who lived in the wilderness far from medical care used chanting and other yogic techniques to maintain their health. For more than 70,000 years, shamans worldwide have sung medicine songs to cure the afflicted, a practice that continues in indigenous cultures today. The Apache people tell a creation story that describes how the art of healing came into the world when people were given the first song.[4] In ancient Egypt, sound was considered so sacred and powerful that chanting and singing were used for two purposes only—to maintain optimal health and high levels of consciousness, and to cut, shape, and lift stone![5]

Eastern spiritual traditions have a long history of healing through the sound of one's own voice. The Bön tradition of Tibet is one of the world's oldest such lineages, predating Buddhism by many thousands of years. Bön lineage holder Tenzin Wangyal Rinpoche describes the healing power of our voice this way:

> We know that in . . . acupuncture, when a needle is placed in a part of the body, it sends a vibration or message to another part or an organ, which causes balance and healing. . . . In a similar way, the vibration of sound as it reverberates on the lips, in the head, and in the chest can affect the body and organs in a very healing way. As the health is affected, so the higher forms of consciousness—emotions, mind, spiritual practice—are also affected. If you are chanting the syllable RAM for the fire element, for example, that vibration is going to open particular channels and chakras, which will affect certain organs, in turn giving a particular experience of higher consciousness.[6]

Traditional Chinese Medicine (TCM) also advocates vocal toning to stimulate and tone the bodily organs. Qi gong master Mingtong Gu tells us that each organ system "has a unique energy structure, vibration, and movement." By intoning certain sounds, he says, we can creatively shift the energetic vibrations in organs to harmonize with the "field of Infinite Potential. . . . This new energetic movement opens up our potential for greater physical and emotional health. As it opens our energy to the spiritual dimensions, we often feel spacious, spontaneous and luminous . . . we are no longer fragmented, and our energy has become integrated with the Oneness."[7]

In other words, by tuning our organs with our voice, we can tune in to the entire cosmos. I will say more on this later.

FOUNTAIN OF YOUTH

Whenever I see a group of students for the first time, I can instantly tell who sings a lot. When I share this with them, they often exclaim in surprise and ask me how I know. There is radiance and openness in the face, a subtle light in the eyes, and a relaxed, attentive expression. Singing also tones the facial muscles. By exercising more than a hundred muscles in the face, regular singing or chanting can give us a musical facelift!

So if you were looking for the Fountain of Youth, making any intentional sound and chanting (which usually involves words) would be a great place to start. A study conducted by the Levine School of Music in Washington, DC, determined that singing in choirs significantly reduces the symptoms of aging in senior populations. Results showed that these seniors—even those more than eighty years old—experienced improvement in eyesight and reduced incidence of depression, had fewer falls and other injuries, and required less medication and fewer visits to doctors. The participants in these studies also attributed a general feeling of greater well-being and overall health, easier breathing, better posture, and a more youthful speaking voice to the singing.[8]

Can singing really improve our health? The answer is *yes*. I've seen singing benefit many of my students, and there's excellent clinical research that confirms my observations. Here's how singing helps us.

First of all, when we sing we have to engage our breath. This alone encourages us to breathe more deeply and strengthens the abdominal muscles, diaphragm, and lungs. Breathing deeply improves our aerobic capacity and helps bring more oxygen to the blood, increasing circulation in the body and providing energy for nearly every function that keeps us alive.

Mitchell L. Gaynor, MD, is a leading oncologist who uses sound and singing in his clinical practice. In his illuminating book, *The Healing Power of Sound,* he cites studies of how simply listening to music produces a score of less obvious— though equally beneficial—physiological responses such as:

lowered anxiety, heartbeat, and respiratory rate

reduced cardiac complications

lowered blood pressure

increased levels of immune-cell messenger molecules that help regulate the activity of other immune cells

drop in stress hormones that activate our body's fight-or-flight response

boost in endorphins, "the brain's natural painkillers," which in turn help build a stronger immune system[9]

Dr. Gaynor's original work represents an exciting new model for Western allopathic medicine that allows for the inclusion of complementary modalities to treat the whole human being, not just a person's symptoms. He offers us this valuable perspective from his decades of work helping people recover from life-threatening illness:

"There is a different medical worldview emerging, one that is holistic rather than compartmentalized. This new medical worldview accepts that . . . our biology cannot simply be reduced to genetic switches

being turned off and on, because virtually
every bodily action occurs simultaneously
with thoughts, feelings, hormonal changes,
immune system modifications, the release of
neurotransmitters and neuropeptides, changes
in cell receptors, fluctuations in biologic
energies, and countless other transformations.
Moreover, we are now learning that these
changes are remarkably coordinated, that
biological systems once thought to be separate
are in constant communication, that genes
regulate certain functions but that thoughts,
feelings, and social experiences can actually
alter gene expression.[10]

We have known for a long time that the mind has the power
to correct physiological imbalances. Now that knowledge is
enhanced with the awareness of the undeniable potential of
singing and music to support healing.

I had the honor of spending time with Dr. Gaynor and shar-
ing the latest research in the field of singing and integrative
medicine. It was a delight to hear my music playing in the
background of his uptown Manhattan office. With enthusi-
asm, he confided to me his vision that there will be a day when
toning and singing with Tibetan and crystal bowls will be
offered in hospitals and health centers everywhere as a healing
option to support the treatment and recovery from life-threatening illnesses. Mitch sings like an angel, and his whole body
resonates like a bell as his calm voice utters inspired words for
health and comfort.

Can you imagine all physicians having the option to give
vibrational prescriptions instead of just chemical remedies? For
me, it would be a dream come true: medicine that reflects the
union of science and heart by means of devotional sound.

FAST TRACK TO RELAX

For this next section, it's helpful to have a little primer on how our nervous systems work. We're going to talk about how singing has proven to be an effective way to influence the autonomic nervous system—the part of the nervous system that regulates involuntary action, such as that of the intestines, heart, and glands.

The two components that make up the autonomic nervous system are the sympathetic nervous system, which accelerates the heart rate, constricts blood vessels, and raises blood pressure, and the parasympathetic nervous system, which slows the heart rate, increases digestive and glandular activity, and relaxes the muscles. The sympathetic nervous system gets activated in times of stress and triggers the release of stress hormones including adrenaline and cortisol. This in turn triggers the classic "fight-or-flight" response, gets us ready for action, tenses our muscles, raises our blood pressure and heart rate, and enables us to fight any saber-toothed tigers that happen to cross our path.

In contrast to this is the well-documented "relaxation response," a term, according to Gaynor, originally coined by cardiologist Herbert Benson, MD, whose clinical studies at Harvard University in the late 1960s revealed that meditation-centered practices could reverse the body's natural fight-or-flight response triggered by chronic or severe stress. Benson found that the subjects' muscles released, respiration and heart rate slowed, and blood pressure decreased. The brain waves took on a distinctive pattern characteristic of relaxation. He also discovered that "eliciting the relaxation response not only caused beneficial physical changes, it actually relieved the symptoms of serious physical ailments and helped promote healing."[11]

Benson also discovered that many different modalities (such as yoga, chanting, and visualization) could also prompt the relaxation response. Since those early studies, researchers have been fascinated to see how sound and music might fit into the healing equation. Research has confirmed that even *listening* to certain music can effectively and rapidly elicit the relaxation response and bring about chemical, hormonal, and cellular changes that actively promote healing.[12]

Real life can sometimes be more compelling than a research paper, however. Like the time one of my students—a woman devoted to her daily singing practice—told me about taking her dog, Mica, for an emergency visit to the vet. The dog was bleeding from the mouth, and my student feared that she was finally succumbing to the lymphoma she had been diagnosed with a year earlier. The bleeding turned out to be unrelated to the cancer and was taken care of with a few stitches, but the vet was astonished to discover that the dog's tumors had completely and inexplicably disappeared—something she'd never seen before and could only attribute to the chemotherapy medication she had prescribed. However, my student had stopped giving Mica the prescribed medicine after only four months. When I asked her what she thought happened, she smiled and said, "It must be all the singing!" She added that every time she took out her harmonium to start her singing practice, Mica would run to sit by her "like her life depended on it . . . and maybe it did." Mica didn't need a prescription; her reliable animal instincts were already leading her to the medicine she needed.

So maybe listening to singing saved the life of my student's four-footed friend, but what does that have to do with us?

The human ear is connected to virtually every organ in the body by means of the tenth cranial—or vagus—nerve. In Latin, *vagus* means "wanderer," and that is a good description of these nerves that travel on both the right and left sides of the body all the way from the head down to the abdominal region. Our wandering vagus nerve is stimulated by sound that enters the auditory canal of the outer ear. The activity of this nerve directly stimulates our parasympathetic nervous system. It carries incoming information from the nervous system to the brain and sends outgoing information that regulates heartbeat, muscle movement, breathing, digestion, and more.

The vagus nerve carries *75 percent* of all parasympathetic activity—the signals that tell our body it is okay to rest and digest. When it is stimulated by soothing sounds—and particularly when we sing—we are sending a message of calm and relaxation to every part of our body. So when we say that something is "music to our ears," it's actually so much more. It's a massage for every organ in the body.

It's no wonder that experts are increasingly looking to sound and music as a fast track to the much sought-after relaxation response. Our own singing voice is the best masseuse we know—and we don't even have to pay for an appointment.

If simply listening to music can produce such a bounty of positive physiological responses, imagine how our bodies might respond when the musical instrument is our own voice. Vocal sounds are a primary source of energy for balancing and stimulating the brain. As the fabric of breath, vibration, and emotion, the singing voice affects the body and mind faster and more efficiently than any other form of sound.

SAY YES TO NO

Composer, naturopathic doctor, and author John Beaulieu has done significant research on how vibration applied to the body through tuning forks impacts the human body on a cellular level. His studies show that applying tuning forks to the body rapidly spikes the production of nitric oxide (NO), a tiny gas molecule fundamental to all life and essential for the healthy function of all organ systems.[13] (Nitric oxide should not be confused with nitrous oxide, the anesthetic commonly called "laughing gas.") Beaulieu suggests that chanting can have a similar effect on stimulating the NO cycle.

The discovery of the crucial role of nitric oxide in promoting the health of the cardiovascular and nervous systems caused the journal *Science* to name it "Molecule of the Year" in 1992. The three American scientists who investigated nitric oxide won a Nobel Prize six years later.[14] They found that when a body is under stress, nitric oxide production diminishes and can result in lack of energy, joint pain, depression, decreased sexual drive, headaches, memory loss, and poor digestion. Over time, these conditions can escalate into major diseases, including cardio-vascular disease, diabetes, Alzheimer's disease, autoimmune diseases, and cancer.

Nitric oxide literally puffs us up—it is so completely intrin-sic to our health on a cellular level. Immune, vascular, and neural cells release NO in six-minute puffing cycles that are closely linked with the activity of the autonomic nervous system. "During the three-minute rising phase of puffing, NO is released and signals the body to move into a parasympa-thetic mode causing cells to relax, move further apart, thin their walls, and become rounder," according to Beaulieu. "During the falling puffing phase, NO dissipates and signals the body to move into sympathetic mode, causing cells to go on alert, cluster together, thicken their cell walls, and become asymmetrical."[15] This puffing cycle allows NO to do its job of destroying viruses, bacteria, and free radicals (molecules responsible for aging and tissue damage).

When nitric oxide production is stimulated, it sets off a cas-cade of beneficial physiological events, which we experience as:

enhanced cell vitality, vascular flow, and heart healing

a stronger immune system and increased ability to prevent and fight infections

more resistance to stress and greater levels of energy and stamina

sharper mental clarity and diminished states of depression
due to the balancing of the autonomic nervous system

improved digestion and natural cleansing

The three Nobel Prize winners determined that nitric oxide
is a vasal dilater that effectively facilitates flow of blood
throughout our body. NO concentrations in our sinuses are
exceptionally high, where its antifungal and antibacterial
properties come in particularly handy. Further studies show
that NO production from inhaling through the nose leads to
a ten- to fifteen-percent increase in the oxidation of the blood,
and that humming increases nasal nitric oxide fifteen- to
twenty-fold.[16] So just humming can improve our circulatory
health, our immunity, and set us on the parasympathetic path
to rest and relaxation.

I can actually see (and hear) the effect of the NO puff
whenever I hold a pair of tuning forks close to someone's ear.
Without fail, the sound of the tuning forks produces a deep
sigh and a spontaneous *ahhh* of release from the person. This
naturally open sound is actually the perfect point of entry to
singing. This is why we say *yes* to NO.

Multivitamin for the Brain

Remember Dr. Benson and his pioneering work regarding the
relaxation response during the 1960s? Well, about the same
time, something strange was happening to the monks at a
Benedictine abbey in France. Nobody could explain why these
men, notorious for their ability to labor tirelessly for long
hours on very little sleep, were suddenly overcome by fatigue,
depression, and illness. Experts who were called in to observe
the monks proposed various remedies—such as changing their
sleeping patterns and abandoning their regular vegetarian
diet—that only made the problem worse. As a last resort, the

monks consulted with Dr. Alfred Tomatis, the physician who brought our attention to the magic of the fetal ear.

It was Dr. Tomatis who recognized that when the monastery's new abbot, a young reformist eager to adopt changes, eliminated chanting from the monks' daily routine, he also took away a vital nutrient: sound. By the time Tomatis visited the monastery, he noted that "seventy of the ninety monks were slumped in their cells like wet dishrags."[17] Within a few months after the doctor began treatment for reawakening their ears, including reviving their practice of chanting for six to eight hours a day, the monks were back to normal—devoting their lives to work and prayer, refreshed after sleeping their customary three to four hours per night. Dr. Tomatis's discoveries that the ear is the "battery of the brain," and that singing can actively charge the brain with frequencies vital to our health and well-being, has forever changed the way we view the human brain.[18]

Gregorian chants, such as those sung by the monks, contain all the frequencies of the voice spectrum, from roughly 70 cycles per second up to 9,000 cycles per second, but within a very different envelope from that of the normal speech. These frequencies, rich in overtones, stimulate our brain, revitalize our cognitive functions, and bestow bountiful benefits to both the chanteur (the one who sings) and anyone who listens. Gregorian chants also awaken consciousness—inducing concentration and sharpening the capacity for self-awareness. If you want to hear the haunting beauty of these chants and witness their healing potential, check out the film *Of Gods and Men,* a touching drama about an order of Trappist monks living in Algeria.

TAKE YOUR EARS TO THE GYM

One of the discoveries that Dr. Tomatis brought to light was that the sounds that enter our ears actually stimulate and fuel our brain—especially the high-frequency sounds rich with over-tones that occur when we sing. When a pitch is played, the main note heard is the fundamental (the note itself), but present also is a series of other pitches above it called overtones or harmonics. The relative strength or weakness of these overtones determines the tone color or timbre of the pitch. The voice of each person produces a different range of overtones or harmonics simultane-ously. That is why all our voices sound different.

There's a wonderful documentary you can watch called *The Music Instinct: Science and Song* (see the resources section for more information) that illustrates this process in detail and with stunning images.

In a very simplified version, our middle ear is the home to three tiny bones (or ossicles) you might remember learning about in school: the hammer, the anvil, and the stirrup, also known by their Latin names as the *malleus,* the *incus,* and the *stapes,* respectively. Attached to the ossicles we find the busiest muscles in our entire body—the tensor tympani and the tiny stapedius—whose job it is to protect the sensitive inner ear from excessive sound. These hard-working muscles never stop, even after we take our last breath. In fact, just as our hearing is the first of our senses to become fully functional in the womb, the sounds we hear are also our last sensory experience as we pass from life.

It's actually possible for these muscles to get out of shape, however, due to childhood ear infections or trauma that causes us to figuratively "shut down our ears." When this happens, the sound no longer reaches the fancy mechanism in our inner ear known as the cochlea, which translates the sound into elec-trical signals that inform and fire up our brain. By singing, we actually tone up those tiny muscles at the same time we feed our brain the most wholesome power bar it could have.

Our ears also house the vestibular system, the unifying system in our brain. The vestibular system is in charge of ori-enting us in space and time, enabling us to stand upright and to know the difference between up and down, right and left, forward and backward. Located in the inner ear, the vestibular system modifies and coordinates information received from our other senses and controls posture, balance, awareness of our body in space, and movement, revealing that the organs for sound and movement are interconnected. A healthy vestibular system is essential to how we orient ourselves in the world and provides the foundation for all higher cognitive functions such as reading, writing, and thinking.

Verticality (or standing upright) is the first step toward human listening and speech, according to Tomatis. This act is controlled by the vestibular system. To understand how connected our vestibular system is to our organs of vocal production, we need only watch the progress of a baby as she wrestles with gravity to take her first tenuous steps all on her own. "First steps lead to first speech," as the saying goes. It is not until the child can negotiate a fully upright posture that the first words come tumbling out.[19]

Dr. Tomatis made another important contribution to the field: that we hear not only through our ears (air conduction), but also via bone conduction. Bone conduction is a primary way of exercising the vestibular system, thereby improving body awareness, posture, and higher-level functioning. More than any other sound, our own singing voice stimulates this system by reverberating throughout all the bony cavities in our cranium, sternum, and chest.

Various listening programs based on the work of Dr. Tomatis have been developed in the last two decades. These programs use specially treated and filtered classical music to improve sensory/motor skills, reading and auditory processing, learning, comprehension, and attention. Through awakening the listening capacity of the ears, retrieving lost frequencies, and exercising the vestibular system, Tomatis-based auditory stimulation programs have been strikingly successful in helping children and adults who suffer from autism, obsessive compulsive disorder

(OCD), attention deficit hyperactivity disorder (ADHD), dyslexia, and other learning or processing difficulties.

Singing (which is often used in conjunction with auditory stimulation programs), does many of the same things for all of us: it wakes up our ears, enhances our listening, stimulates our brain with energy, and calms and strengthens our foundational vestibular system, opening pathways to higher-level functioning.

SINGING TO CHANGE THE BRAIN

Over the last few decades, researchers have embraced the daring proposition that music and singing have the capacity to literally change our brains. Daniel Levitin, a former record producer and professional musician whose fascination with music and the brain led him to embrace a career in neuroscience, is at the forefront of this research. In his remarkable book, *The World in Six Songs: How the Musical Brain Created Human Nature,* he tells the story of music and its primacy in shaping human nature. "Through a process of co-evolution of brains and music, through the structures throughout our cortex and neocortex . . . from the limbic system to the cerebellum, music uniquely insinuates itself into our heads."[20]

One of the most significant and exciting advances in the science of the brain in the last forty years is neuroplasticity, the idea that the brain can reorganize itself by forming new neural connections throughout life. Neuroplasticity refers to the ability of the brain and nervous system in all species to change structurally and functionally as a result of input from the environment.

The founders of Integrated Listening Systems, a Tomatis-based program that uses specially treated music to help build new neural pathways, describe how neuroplasticity works: "For example, if one hemisphere of the brain is damaged, the intact hemisphere may take over some of its functions. The brain compensates for damage in effect by reorganizing and forming new connections between intact neurons. In order to reconnect, the neurons need to be stimulated through activity. The same is true for parts of the brain compensating for injury or disease."[21] Our capacity for neuroplasticity, therefore, makes it literally possible to "rewire" the brain to make it work better.

Musician, composer, and neuroscientist Mark Tramo, sheds light on why music can be such an effective tool in changing our brain. He states, "A human brain is divided into two hemispheres, and the right hemisphere has been traditionally identified as the seat of music appreciation. However, no one has found a 'music center' there, or anywhere else."[22]

Tramo goes on to speak of studies revealing that music perception emerges from the interplay of activity in both sides of the brain.

> Some brain circuits respond specifically to music, but as you would expect, parts of these circuits participate in other forms of sound processing. For example, the region of the brain dedicated to perfect pitch is also involved in speech perception. . . . The right side of the cortex is crucial for perceiving pitch as well as certain aspects of melody, harmony, timbre, and rhythm. . . . The left side of the brain in most people excels at processing rapid changes in frequency and intensity, both in music and words.[23]

With so many centers in the brain lighting up at once, it is no wonder that music is potent brain medicine.

One of my favorite movies in recent years is *The King's Speech,* based on the true story of King George VI's unexpected ascension to the English throne, despite a debilitating speech impediment that led him to the door of an unorthodox speech therapist. During a climactic, emotional scene, the therapist has the king singing what his crippling stammer won't allow him to express in words. Through some alchemical brain magic, the king is able to eloquently sing his deepest feelings to the tune of "Camptown Races"—*doo-da, doo-da!*

My direct personal experience supports the research that humming, toning, and singing simple, familiar melodies can promote and support a healthy brain, optimizing its capacity and even restoring functions that have been lost.

Recently, I had an intimate encounter with how singing can restore impaired brain function. At the age of ninety-four, my mother had a stroke and suffered severe aphasia (the loss of ability to communicate both verbally and in writing). It was heartbreaking to see her locked inside her body with no means of conveying her most fundamental needs. She was famous in our community for her lively storytelling skills, and she loved tangos and children's songs. By singing these simple melodies, we were able to bypass the damaged left-brain region and converse joyfully through song, with me adapting the lyrics to whatever needed to be communicated. My mom's habitually joyful nature reasserted itself as she was able to articulate some essential words, share her healthy brain, and be understood.

In these tender interactions with my mother, I was actually employing a therapeutic modality called Melodic Intonation Therapy (MIT),[24] which I had used frequently in my previous career as a music psychotherapist. This type of therapy is now widely implemented for language recovery after a stroke or brain injury has damaged the left brain. MIT uses the musical elements of speech, such as melody and rhythm, to improve expressive language. By utilizing singing (which remains a preserved function), this technique engages language-capable regions in the undamaged right hemisphere of the brain.

In addition to the MIT protocol, call-and-response singing that uses short songs and simple melodies proves to be another excellent way to improve memory, coordination, cerebral function, and health. A great deal of research demonstrates that live and pre-recorded singing of familiar music is also very effective in improving memory and communication with Alzheimer's patients. The best part of my former clinical practice as a musical psychotherapist was to see how singing would help these patients connect immediately with healthy memories and eagerly sing along.

Research continues to pour in on how different types of music can restore or enhance brain function for patients with Alzheimer's and dementia, motor and speech disorders such as Parkinson's disease, and for those who, like my mother, suffer from aphasia. Other research continues to explore how and which kinds of music can rewire the brain to promote learning and cognitive improvement.

I invite you to visit the resources section at the end of this book if you'd like to learn more about this fascinating topic, as research in the field evolves and abounds. For now, we trust the neuroscientists to figure out how this all works while we sing.

exercise 2   Recharging the Brain

These practices, individually or in sequence, stimulate the brain and promote mental clarity. Repeating these exercises often enhances tone memory and expands vocal range.

Inward Humming—With eyes closed, gently hum on any single tone or note that is comfortable for you. Tighten and push the lips slightly forward with sustained pressure, and pull the sound upward toward the crown of the head. Continue for three to four minutes, noticing where you feel the vibrations in your body. Resting in silence, let yourself become aware of any differences in your physical or mental body.

Scanning—Starting with a low-pitched hum deep in your belly, let the tone rise and fall in pitch as the hum moves up and down your spine. Think of sliding slowly up the scale as the sound moves from your belly all the way to the top of your head. Take a smooth breath at the top and slide back down. Accompany the motion of the hum with slight movements of the hands and arms, moving them slowly up and down in front of the body, tracing the raising and lowering of the pitch. Repeat as many times as you like. Afterward, rest in the vibrant silence.

Bullroarer—A bullroarer is a primitive Australian instrument made of wood and string that makes a roaring sound when whirled in a circle over the head or in front of the body. Moving your arm in a circular motion, let your voice follow the movement with an energized close-lipped *mum*. Let the pitch and volume respond to the movement of the body.

Observe your energy level and how your body feels both before and after each of these practices. Listening to the silence afterward is the key.

Transforming Emotions

It's easy to get drawn into all the latest scientific information about why singing is good for you. But I don't want you to forget one of the most important things: that singing just feels great. Using your voice by toning, chanting, or singing a jazz tune can make you feel more balanced and shift your energy field more efficiently than anything you may have in your medicine chest.

During my years as a music psychotherapist, I witnessed over and over again that singing your pain is as effective—or even more effective—than talking about it. Yes, singing expresses emotions, although the truly liberating aspect lies in the transformation of personal feelings into universal emotions that occurs with the conscious use of vibration when we sing. Distressing emotions carry constraint and rigidity, and they sometimes crystallize into physical pain or other bodily symptoms. Freeing our voice through song and chant also frees our body and our heart—giving us a creative way to release the tension of these painful, ultimately self-centered emotions. Singing can shape and pacify emotions like an artist sculpts a piece of clay.

The human voice has always been an essential instrument for personal and communal expression in times of joy or sorrow, rage or fear. Music therapist Kate Richards Geller, who calls her work Sing for Yourself, describes how singing through strong emotional states for one's own self (rather than for an audience), helps people release physical and psychological blocks, and allows a sense of flow and ease to move in.[25] People who "sing for themselves" show dramatic improvement in their ability to cope with problems, to concentrate and learn new skills, to soothe depressive moods, and to move through troubling emotions.

Geller writes, "The singing, music itself . . . can access our inner resources and support us through a myriad of emotions. The process of moving through these emotions can soothe and renew us—mentally, physically, spiritually, socially—so that we can be open to establishing a new balance and a renewed sense of well-being within ourselves and our communities."[26]

Our voice is our ever-present companion, telling us how we feel, where we're coming from, and how our physical and emotional dispositions are at any particular moment. It is almost impossible to hide feelings and thoughts in the voice, thus the tone and texture of the voice mirror who we are at any moment. As a spiritual practice, singing can help us transcend, or even change, our emotional disposition.

Comfort in Community

Singing promotes healing, not only for individuals but for entire communities. Dr. Joanne Loewy, a distinguished music therapist and the director of the Louis Armstrong Center for Music and Medicine in New York City, works with singing, toning, and chanting in music therapy for post-traumatic stress and pain management. After the World Trade Center disaster, she participated in a large-scale program in which more than thirty professional music therapists in the New York metropolitan area provided thousands of music-therapy interventions over a period of six months to children, adults, caregivers, and families affected by the attacks on the Twin Towers. This musical intervention, mostly singing, helped rebuild a much-needed sense of trust and safety within the community.[27]

I believe that positive human resonance created by communal chanting provides a safe way to access disturbing memories and to support feelings of belonging.

Just as the voice of the individual releases tension and emotional pain, the function of the voice in community is to dissolve boundaries. On most occasions in history when unpredictable calamity strikes, people sing together. And when people sing together, remarkable things occur.

In the summer of 1987, something extraordinary was happening in the tiny country of Estonia, tucked away in a corner of the Soviet Union that juts into the Baltic Sea. People were singing—singing for their freedom.

These people had lived through decades of tyranny, first under the Soviets, then the Nazis, and then the Soviets again. This country, with one of the smallest populations in the world, also has one of the largest treasuries of folk songs and a musical tradition that sustained the people while preserving the Estonian language and culture during these oppressive regimes. Lacking any military strength, these people fought—and won— one of the most courageous battles in history, armed only with their voices and their national pride. It was dubbed The Singing Revolution—if you want to be truly inspired by the sheer power and dignity of the human voice, you can watch the outstanding documentary of the same name.

The Tallinn Song Festival Grounds were the fitting site for the beginning of the revolution, when in June of 1987 more than 10,000 people per night flocked to sing patriotic songs forbidden by the Soviet government. One of the singers recounts the story: "We sang all night and everybody went home early in the morning. It was emotionally so strong that the next day there were even more people. The day after, there were even more people. People took out their hidden flags. They had these flags hidden for fifty years, and now they took these out and started to wave them." On the final night of these protests, more than 200,000 Estonians gathered.[28]

Over the next five years the singing movement, along with other resourceful demonstrations of nonviolent noncooperation, spread through neighboring Baltic states, until the collapse of the Soviet Union in 1991. According to the filmmakers, "The force of the human voice massed in song was the cultural catalyst that awoke, energized, and united the nation of Estonia. It was a political and cultural statement that brought all Estonians together and gave them courage to rebel. After that there was no turning up. . . . A series of clever political maneuvers, combined with ever-growing singing demonstrations, overwhelmed a confused and failing Moscow."[29]

I fully believe that the emotional magic of singing, scientifically applied, will contribute to awakening consciousness and relieving human suffering on a grand scale. These days, we are actually seeing social movements characterized by singing crowds in countries that the media loosely calls "new democracies." Singing is literally re-enchanting the world.

Warming Heart, Melting Mind

I've had many musical careers during my life, but through them all it seems that my official job has been to warm the heart through singing. People often come to see me with the idea that they want a singing lesson, but I've realized over the years that what they really want is permission to open their heart and to have their heart's expression be heard.

The mere vibration created when we sing can break up old patterns of tension, fear, and limiting beliefs. The tension often shows in the throat. There is an understanding in Traditional Chinese Medicine that when the throat center is out of balance, it is considered the stopper, the cork in the bottle between the head and the heart. The conscious use of vibration or singing shakes it loose, freeing the passage of emotions. What your heart wants to say can be sung and come out into the world.

Nicole Becker, owner of the Ojas Yoga and Wellness Center in El Cerrito, California, describes why she uses chanting to open and close every yoga class:

> In yoga, we practice unifying the heart with
> the mind. Imagine the mind is a beehive
> filled with honey, and the heart is a gentle
> flame underneath. When the throat center is
> open, the flame in the heart can reach the
> mind. The fire in the heart softens the mind,
> melting the wax of the beehive so the nectar
> of enlightenment can trickle down from
> the crown into the heart. The light of love
> goes up from the heart, and the sweetness of
> compassion trickles back down. We get to live
> from our heart.[30]

Devotional chanting takes us directly to this place. The practices in this book consistently point to the melting quality in singing. Experiencing this quality softens our mind and transmutes emotional energy, thereby awakening us to our innate joy and self-perfected condition. In the practices, we incorporate subtle motions of the hands and arms to entrain with the movement between the heart and the mind. We spontaneously connect the voice—which loves to go up and down—with the heart that longs to be open, to give, and to receive.

Singing changes us on a physiological and psycho-spiritual level, and it touches our humanity both individually and collectively. Not to mention the fact that singing is the most ancient healing art—it literally puts creativity at the tip of your tongue.

3

Permission to Sing

*It is important that we sing. . . . Singing frees
the soul, makes it flexible, and helps it soar
and expand. Singing lets the sun in—gives
warmth to our lives and wings to our spirit.
Those who sing know this.*

DINA SORESI WINTER, *Singing and the Etheric Tone*

Many people request private lessons with me. In this
context, I often hear, "I can't find my voice" or "My throat
chakra is closed" or "They told me at school that I can't carry
a tune" or "I want to sing, but I'm not a musician." My initial
response to all of these is: "What makes you think this?" Then
I say: "Can you *see* your voice—and if you could, would you
be able to find it?" "Did you put a lid on your throat chakra?"
"Is a tune too heavy for you to carry?" "Did the birds go to
music school?"

I realize that when people come to me they're really seeking
permission to use their voice, permission to express themselves, permission to sing. The following chapters provide

a gentle and accessible method for anyone to develop the voice and let it soar free. The emphasis is on *freeing* the voice, rather than *finding* it. It was never lost.

Singing is an opportunity to regain personal freedom. This is the first thing I share with students of singing, or those who come with any voice-related issue, along with the advice, "First feel free." These three dynamic "Fs" make a strong impact on the mind and set our course as we embark on a regular practice of singing and opening the voice. I heard this advice myself many times from the notable Tibetan Dzogchen master Chögyal Namkhai Norbu in the context of teachings about ancient practices of self-liberation. The spontaneous expressive nature of the voice intrinsically carries a promise of self-liberation.

"Sing as an offering." This is my second piece of advice. The intention to sing comes from abundance—the voice has so much to communicate and express. When singing becomes an offering, we discover the antidote to any kind of performance anxiety. There is no longer any need to fear standing in front of an audience that will scrutinize the singer to the end of her toes.

I like the rhyme in my third piece of advice: "Singing is beauty, not duty." This principle emerges as an uplifting reminder when we follow the previous advice. The more we sing, the more we come to realize that singing is creative expression—an art form. The art of singing doesn't require much effort, but it does rely on our capacity to appreciate beauty, to be carried away by it, and to convey it in each tone.

The singing voice is the most delicate ingredient in the vibrational formula that makes music such a magnificent healing art. Those who sing deserve support, credit, patience, and recognition.

I'm inspired by this passage from *The Musical Life: Reflections on What It Is and How to Live It* by composer, author, and master teacher, W. A. Mathieu, known to his friends and colleagues as Allaudin.

It is a wonderful thing to hear the beauty in
another's voice and let that person know it.
When you hear the depth or longing in your
friend's voice as something true and good,
point that out, be a kind mirror. You are not
only helping her, you are helping yourself
hear your own voice in a positive light. That
goodness you hear in your friend's voice is in
yours also.[1]

I used to drive more than fifty miles to Allaudin's farm every
week for my music lesson. He helped the eyes in my ears see the
beauty first. No wonder he remains one of the most inspiring
and treasured teachers of our time.

It's clear to me that this is the reason I have a constant flow
of students; as soon as I hear the beauty in someone's voice, I
can't keep myself from pointing it out. When I hear fear or pain
in someone's voice, I accompany the feeling and make music out
of it. Together we embark on a journey of creative expression
using the language of cries, clamors, and lamentations until
we cross the threshold from the impeded to the unrestricted
voice. The art of freeing the voice has an alchemical influence
on the emotions, allowing us to approach fear, sorrow, or any
other painful feeling as musical moods that can be expressed,
released, and transformed through sound.

In this chapter, I offer ideas for creating the external and
internal conditions to develop a successful vocal practice. My
hope is that in these pages you will grow in appreciation of
human resonance and the alchemical properties of sound. This
will give you permission to use your voice freely. More than
permission to sing, may this book provide you with a healthy
prescription to sing as often as you can.

CULTIVATING FAMILIARITY

The concept of "practice" can sound scary to some of us. Whenever I can, I like to express this idea with one of my favorite expressions from His Holiness the XIV Dalai Lama: "cultivate familiarity." It's essential to cultivate familiarity with our voice and to really get to know the path of development we are choosing. The path includes how to listen, acceptance of how we sound now, and how we want to sound. This is best accomplished by doing the same series of exercises as often as possible, whenever we practice.

Fundamental to our progress is listening and learning how to sustain our attention in the practice we are doing without jumping from one thing to another. The aim of Yoga of the Voice is to build a safe container. When I use the word *yoga,* I am talking about the fulfillment of doing the same routine every time and creating the time to do it often. The idea is to memorize a series of practices and chants, to become very familiar with them, and to spend at least twenty-one minutes a day doing them.

There is always one student in every class who asks me, "Why twenty-one minutes?" Several years ago, I participated in a scientific study on the effect of microtonal chanting on brain waves. The other participants were yogis, musicians, Tibetan monks, meditators, and others who use their contemplative practices to enter a state of expanded consciousness and elation. Across the board, the magic number was twenty-one. After twenty-one minutes, the brain-wave patterns of all the practitioners, no matter what their level of practice, shifted into a relaxed, theta-wave state. So it was determined that twenty-one minutes is a good length of time for beginners to establish that sense of continuum, that "groove of the mind" that we call practice. The Tibetan monks, of course, needed only about three minutes to shift their brain waves into a spacious theta state.

By dwelling in uninterrupted vocal practice for at least twenty-one minutes, we allow for progressive resonance with the entire range of colors and tones in our voice. The intention is to establish some kind of order so we feel safe and sound in the home of our tone. It is important to find a sequence of practices and stick to them. This proves to be the way to mastery of all practices that have a yogic nature. The more you do the same, the better you get, the deeper your confidence, and the more your practice evolves into a spiritual path. If we constantly experiment with new practices, we might have fun and enjoy the freedom, but we are actually less free when we step outside of the container. We put the fruition of our practice at risk.

When we become comfortable with what we are doing and how we are doing it, we always have a place of safety, a still and neutral place to return to in the midst of changing circumstances. When we feel safe because we've been making music, chanting, or doing a contemplative practice with sound, self-expression comes naturally. The voice opens. We feel free first!

BUILDING A CHANTING REFUGE

You might consider creating a private "music temple"—a small corner in your home where you gather musical instruments, books, recordings, and pictures. This temple is always ready for singing and for connecting with sound as healing energy; it's a pleasing place for your voice and your practices. This will become the nest for nurturing the "bird" in your voice. Even if your voice is a soaring eagle, it still appreciates a place to rest.

The instruments you bring into your sanctuary will become your allies: drones, bells, drums, shakers, Tibetan bowls, iPhone apps, tuning forks, chopsticks, water jugs. When you use your imagination the list is endless. Consider seriously investing in some kind of a drone—any musical instrument that can produce a sustained pitch, arpeggio, or chord—such as a *tamboura,* an

Indian *raagini* box, or a harmonium. A CD or digital download of a drone works well too, and it can accompany you in your car and everywhere you go. A favorite of my students is the *sruti* box (or *surpeti*; pronounced "shruti"), a small wooden instrument with reeds that produces a rich drone the voice can't resist—and that you can learn to play in a few minutes. See the resources section at the end of the book to find out where to get them.

Perhaps you could make an altar in your chanting sanctuary and decorate it with sacred objects: a photo of you with your teacher, a journal, this book—anything that reminds you that you are safe in musical space. Dedicate this space and use it to cultivate familiarity with your yogic voice. Remember to be graceful and grateful and, at the end of each day, it's beneficial to dedicate the merit of your practice to all sentient beings.

Your sanctuary should be the place you come to practice daily or as often as possible. You can start by creating a sacred sound to dedicate your sacred space with a practice called The Primordial Sound. This practice uses the sound *Hu*, which is considered the original sound in the most ancient traditions. In the words of Sufi mystic Hazrat Inayat Khan:

> The sound Hu is the most sacred: the mystics
> of all ages called it Ismi-Azam, the name of the
> most High, for it is the origin and end of every
> sound as well as the background of each word.
> The word Hu is the spirit of all sounds and of all
> words and is hidden under them all, as the spirit
> in the body. It does not belong to any language,
> but no language can help belonging to it.[2]

Using minimal opening of the lips, this Hu sound requires no effort to produce, so it promotes perfect ease in the body. Listen to the audio and then do the following exercise to practice Hu.

(▶) Listen to track 1: Primordial Sound: Hu

exercise 3   Primordial Sound: Hu

This is a practice for relaxing the breath, pacifying the mind, and connecting to the mystery within sacred sound.

1. Stand with your weight balanced on both feet or sit comfortably. Tune into your body and be present with your breath.

2. Inhale softly. While exhaling, effortlessly sound the syllable *hu* (pronounced "heeoo" with a breathy H) with your lips shaped like a kiss, turning your focus to the vibration on your lips.

3. Keep intoning this sound until you feel your attention completely immersed in the dimension of sound.

SINGING WITH A DRONE

A drone is a continuous tone that establishes a harmonic center. It can be a single long note or, the way we usually work with it, a chord that consists of the tonic (or root tone) and the fifth note above the tonic (the dominant), or the tonic and the fourth. Depending on what instrument is playing it, the drone will involve many overtones and partial harmonies, making the sound thin or rich. Other key aspects include extended duration, modular repetition, and control of volume.

Drones make the perfect accompaniment for establishing a tonal landscape upon which a composition can be built. The drone has always been an essential element of the classical music of India, where it is typically played by the tamboura. Great masters call the sound of the tamboura *"ash,"* a word that evokes the echoes of the breath of God. To me, the drone recalls the eternal voice of the universe.

(▶)   Listen to track 2: A Drone for Your Practice

You can use the accompanying ten-minute audio track as a drone for your practice. The drone is composed of the tones of a sruti box, a tamboura, and strings. You may use this recording for any practice or exercise that calls for a drone.

Effectively, a drone is a harmonic current of sound that can be generated by any instrument. As a musician, I find it extremely gratifying to create drones with as many instruments as I encounter: guitar, harmonium, piano, flute, viola, and cello. The didgeridoo, of course, is the granddaddy of drones. We can create drones with almost anything: all we have to do is rub our hands together with a continuous, even motion and we produce a drone. The hum of a fan, an air conditioner, the sound of rain, and distant traffic are all examples of drone sounds.

There are fantastic natural drones everywhere. A highly recommended sound meditation is to go out and listen to the drones in nature. As a Mills College graduate student who recorded music late into the night, I would often go outside and lie on the lawn to listen to and improvise with the steady chorus of frogs croaking raucously in the pond. Listening to the immensely rich and sustained overtonal symphony of those frogs later inspired me to write a mini-opera, entitled *The Frog Monks*. Perhaps you have your own drone serenade story?

Why do we need a drone? In music, a drone always shows us where "home" is. *The drone is the throne of the voice.* It's a royal resting place for the voice to land and breathe between melodic passages. When we chant with a drone, the voice embarks on a journey with tone: dwelling on the fundamental tone of the drone (or the root tone), slowly departing from it, diving into subtle undulations, and wandering through transformations of timbre and texture. Eventually, the tone returns home, and the voice is open.

How we listen is crucial. Singing with the drone is an opportunity to change our minds and our hearts. The steady, unchangeable tone and its quality of "hovering over time" lead us, as listeners, into a meditation-like state and slowly clear the mind of thought and emotion. We are cultivating a posture of the mind that allows for sound to follow breath, and voice to follow sound. As we master the art of singing with drones, we fine-tune our auditory perception and tune our voice as a musical instrument.

The art of droning—playing with long tones—is a powerful tool for voice development, and it's instrumental in the therapeutic dimension as well. Droning can have an instantaneous effect on emotional disposition by releasing tension and relaxing body and mind. It can also enhance the self-confidence of our sometimes critical inner musician. Because droning stabilizes energy and increases listening and receptive capacity, I recommend it for children with learning disabilities and for mentally or emotionally challenged patients. And of course, droning is wonderful for absolutely everyone on Planet Music.

(▷) Listen to track 3: Create Your Own Drone

exercise 4 Creating a Drone

This practice will ignite your creative imagination and increase your appreciation of the world of the drone. The accompanying audio track demonstrates some kitchen drones as well as drones we hear in nature, such as the sounds of wind and the ocean.

1. Go into your kitchen and see how many types of drones you can make with the "instruments" you find there. Try turning on the blender, running water, starting the coffee machine. What can you do with the whir of a salad spinner combined with the refrigerator hum?

2. Play with layering the drones and enjoy the symphony.

(▶) Listen to track 4: Singing to Disappear

exercise 5 Singing to Disappear

This practice involves toning with an external drone—moving and modulating slowly and subtly—to enhance deep listening and concentration. As you experiment, your voice will "disappear" into the sound of the drone. The audio download demonstrates this practice.

1. Listening to the drone, get familiar with the root tone. Then softly begin to match the root of the drone using the sound of *ah, oo,* or a hum with relaxed breath. The goal is to match your voice with the drone until it sounds like one voice.

2. Allow yourself to become immersed in the experience of opening the voice, departing from the root tone, diving into subtle undulations of the same tone, and wandering through minimal transformations of timbre and texture.

3. Keep your phrasing simple, calm, and knowing. The tone always returns "home"—to the infinite tonal ground offered by the drone.

Dharana: The Flashlight of Attention

We can think of consciousness as a flashlight: whatever we point at with the beam will light up. First, we need to decide what it is in ourselves we want to shine the light on, and then gently illuminate it. This requires a special kind of focus. In yoga, this is referred to as *dharana,* or single-pointed attention. Dharana is an essential quality of any yoga practice—and the Yoga of the Voice is no exception.

Dharana is fundamental to meditation or any deep contemplative practice in which the mind homes in on one object and bypasses other thoughts or distractions. According to my teacher Khansahib Ali Akbar Khan—considered one of the most accomplished Indian classical musicians and a "national living treasure" in both India and the United States—dharana (or the steady mind of concentration) is the "first challenge and the first friend" in the refinement of our musical capacity.

The tunefulness of your voice is determined by the quality of your attention, the discipline of repetition, and the appreciation of mood. It's a good idea to keep your antenna always tuned to the spirit land, remembering that singing is an offering and an ancient healing art that aims to resonate with the breath of God.

Droning, accompanied with slow melodic movements of the voice, proves to be an excellent preliminary practice to attain and maintain the state of dharana. The following Singing Breath practice uses the sound of *ah* to produce gentle vibrations that help us settle into the voice and stimulate energy flow.

▶ Listen to track 5: Ah: The Singing Breath

exercise 6   Ah: The Singing Breath

This practice relaxes the voice, clears emotions, and creates a feeling of spaciousness. It's good to do it in a quiet room, accompanied, if possible, by a live or recorded drone (such as that on audio track 2) to facilitate your concentration.

1. As you meet and listen to your breath, slowly allow it to become softly audible.

2. Effortlessly start toning on *ahhh* (the breathy sound of "ah" as in "father"). Allow your sound to be slow, clear, sustained, and luminous. When you need to take a breath,

allow the incoming breath to be as relaxed and easy as the toning of *ahhh*.

3. Notice your voice resonating in your chest, and move your hands and arms to usher your pitch slowly and minimally up and down, until you feel *ah* coming from your whole body. Feel free to play with this, noticing how the movement of your hands might alter the pitch or quality of the sound. Eventually, you will become confident in this slow dance of breath, movement, and sound.

4. Dwell in the pauses. Listen. Deeply listen.

5. Abide in the silence you just created in your mind.

In wisdom traditions of sound healing, the sustained sounding of *ah* connects with our primordial potential. It represents our unlimited capacity of awareness and clarity. Everything can arise from it, and thus it's one of the most potent sounds that can be generated by the voice.[3] In the fertile silence after the practice, notice how the breath, along with listening to the drone, leads your mind to a state of heightened sensibility. You have become one with the one tone.

THE TEACHER WITHIN

Your ally in this journey is your teacher: me in these pages—as well as all of my teachers, and their teachers before them—plus all your visible and invisible teachers. The Buddhists have a tradition called Guru Yoga, which literally means union with the guru, or teacher. The actual meaning of the word "guru" in Sanskrit is he who, with the weight of knowledge, is able to disperse darkness. In this fundamental practice, we use sound and visualization to embody the teacher within and become one with the guru. But the guru is not necessarily a person you can see: the guru is the teacher in you, a calm and confident voice within—a seed for personal transformation and a symbol of integration with wholeness. Through a conscious practice that involves sound and visualization, you grow in presence, confidence, and love as the wisdom of the masters becomes inseparable from your own mind. Chanting is the path; the teacher is within. You find that you are never alone on the path.

As you surrender to the guidance of your visible and invisible teachers, your body bows in the posture of *shaddra,* or "unconditional reverence"—the feeling of: *I'm so grateful you taught me this; I will offer this practice to you every time.*

Shaddra is not in itself a yoga posture, but an attitude necessary for the embodiment of the teacher and the practices. For more than twenty-seven years, the most earnestly awaited gesture of my week was to bow and touch my teacher's feet after my *raga* class (raga will be discussed in chapter 7). I felt illuminated by my own innocence—a sense of humbleness, of devotion, and the awareness of being blessed by a master who was giving me everything I ever dreamed of as a musician, without asking for anything in exchange but practice. The best part is that practicing becomes an act of love.

To truly practice Guru Yoga, it is essential to acknowledge with unconditional reverence your teachers and their lineage, to offer gratitude, and to credit them for their influence in your life and art—at all times and without exception.

Before I engage in any singing, I hum softly and visualize all the teachers I have or have had—and I become one with their presence. Everything I know, and everything I want to share with you—from yoga to meditation to freeing the voice—is for and from my teachers, and this liberating art of singing is the fruit of the practice of Guru Yoga, applied in the dimension of music.

We live in a world where we learn more about fragmentation than about wholeness. Through dedicated practice, the presence of our inner teacher makes us feel that we are in safe company, and we become very confident. More and more we realize that through sound we can go beyond divides and feel complete. Even if you have never met the physical teacher, you can find the teachings. In Guru Yoga, it's all inside. The only thing that is required is repetition—mindful repetition of the same: the same practice, the same melody, the same note, *until that becomes the guru.*

Chanting is central to the practice of Guru Yoga, and all of the great wisdom traditions have been transmitting spiritual information through this method. Guru Yoga is a state of pure love and of union with the master, the teachings, and the potential of realizing Oneness.

Your First Assignment: Banning Illegal Language

Before you begin your practice—maybe before you read the next chapter—I invite you to start a journal dedicated to the exploration of your voice. This will become an intimate witness of the journey into sound consciousness on which you are about to embark.

On the first pages, I suggest you write down every pessimistic belief you have about your voice or your ability to sing, such as "I can't sing" or "I'm tone deaf" or "My voice doesn't sound pretty." I want you to look at all the "crazy ideas" you come up with and explore them back to their roots. Observe when those beliefs took hold, and all the "evidence" you collected over the years to support them and give them life.

Spend some time with this. It's vital to identify and demystify personal beliefs about our capacity (or the lack of it) as well as misconceptions about the voice itself. The best way to start is to bring them to the surface. Once you name all the ghosts and demons in the experience of your voice, realize that all the language you've used to write about them is officially illegal language. Anything that starts with "I can't . . ."

or "My voice isn't . . ." falls into this category. On the path of liberation through sound, this illegal language can't ever be used again. This is important!

In the weeks and months to come, as you begin to cultivate familiarity with your precious voice, you must be diligent in eliminating all illegal language from your vocabulary. I invite you to forgive and *dis*member all those old ideas. Remember that your voice is a delicate instrument that needs safety and kindness in order to blossom tunefully, in natural joy and spontaneity.

The Buddha tells us that from the beginning we are pure and perfect. Approach your voice and the experience of singing from your Buddha nature, rejoicing in your innate perfection and innocence. While you're at it, remember that your moody voice loves nothing better than a cup of hot water with honey to keep it moist, uninterrupted, and happy.

4

Our Mystical Instrument

The voice is not only indicative of man's character, it is the expression of his spirit.

HAZRAT INAYAT KHAN, *The Mysticism of Sound and Music*

The voice is a musical instrument made of breath, muscle, and emotion. Through this miraculous instrument, we experience music with our skin, our bones, our body temperature, our pulse. The singing voice connects us with the flow of life gushing through our being at full force.

This voice is the expression of *prana*—our life force. The singing breath is the outward manifestation of prana, it connects the body and the mind, and vibrates the skeletal structure, energizing the surrounding organs and tissues. The singing voice also stimulates prana; the more we sing, the more life force we generate. Singing creates more radiance, more rosy color in the cheeks, more blood circulating happily throughout the body and the brain. So as prana gives and prana receives, life seems to increase.

As effortless sound is made, it relaxes the mind and harmonizes perceptions; unnecessary tensions find release. Even one long note, or one syllable with intent, is enough to bring forth this "freedom" effect. Whether the song is a prayerful call to spirit or a comforting nonverbal melody, the slow sounding of the voice helps to restore vitality and kindle a feeling of well-being and happiness.

Our singing voice connects us with our true energetic and emotional nature. Awakening the whole body of the voice becomes a spiritual path that involves both the body and the mind—with the ultimate destination being the experience of divine radiance and openness.

The Yoga of the Voice path awakens the voice to its highest potential. It is not "vocal training" or a promise of enlightenment through as many octaves of tone production as you can buy. Instead, through it we entrain the heart and engage skillfully with the music, with each other, and with the world of sound.

Here, in the pure dimension of listening, the voice has no ownership, nothing personal—it is simply a musical instrument. We meet our inner musician. In this space there is no singer—only breath, tone, and vibration. The voice is at once music, meditation, and medicine. A whole-istic experience! But in order to experience the true mysticism of sound and music, we first have to demystify some notions we have about the life of the voice.

MUSICAL MATERIALISM

In our Eurocentric musical culture, we tend to approach the voice through a group of notes on a piece of paper. We train our ears to hear the pitch of the notes and the intervals between them. That is good, but we're also told that our voice is either pitched high, medium, or low, as if the voice were a separate mechanism mounted in the body, capable of producing only a certain range of notes. This Western way of thinking about music and musicianship constantly strives for "more."

More Notes

Together with this rather mechanical perception of the voice, great emphasis is given to singing songs that condense lots of information into a short amount of time: fast chords that change quickly through complex harmonies with lots of variation of tone and (often) words. There is little regard to the benefit of preliminary vocal practices before approaching the desired song. Warm-up exercises tend to be fast, encouraging tension and fatigue and inhibiting the integration of mind, body, and spirit. This unwholesome approach to singing is a form of what I call "musical materialism." This view sees the voice as something that needs to be trained rather than opened, and that singers are to be compared, mass-produced, and labeled "Made in China."

In our current musical culture, the student (who *must* learn to read music) is usually challenged to sing with and to imitate a piano, on which each note or key plays separately from the other. In actuality, the human voice vibrates like the string of a viola—with microtonal subtleties. The breath cycle that accompanies the piano-voice practice ends up being short and anxious instead of long and relaxed like the bow on a string. As a result, powerful musical passages are undertaken too quickly and the experience of singing starts to feel like flipping TV channels. This fast-edited, short-attention-span singing makes poor nourishment for the voice's bird spirit.

More Breath

Vocal technique does not have to create tension. In most cases, conventional voice training constricts the breath while it does its best to convince us that we are guilty of not having *enough* breath support. Moreover, it tries to persuade us that this lack of breath support is the cause of poor tone and any other numerous vocal impediments. This is all true, but paradoxically this tense approach to breath support—or lack of it—actually *causes* us to constrict the breath even further and stop singing.

I wonder: is the lack of breath support the cause or the result of the tension generated by that standard practice?

To me, this is like saying, "Don't think about elephants!" As soon as someone tells us that we don't have enough breath support, our natural instinct is to try to muscle up some more. The result is that we experience more effort, more tension. And the tension is actually the problem.

The good singing breath follows the same law as dancing—it is the result of the delicate balance between minimal effort and somatic awareness. We want to summon the breath flow from the muscle of the belly to the lungs, carefully drive it up and down the spine, and gently release it from the throat and the vocal cavity. We spice it up with a slight twist of movement that makes us want more of the same. So let's make more music with the voice—more sensually, more pace-fully—staying observant yet relaxed.

More Money

Finally, our modern culture encourages us to buy music for relaxation, music for concentration, music for babies, music for bathtubs, and more. Ancient traditions remind us that music is not just *for* us; music does something *to* us. The affective power of music can change our world without us having to open our pocketbooks. Music takes us beyond the part that needs to know everything beforehand (and how much it costs) and slips open the door from the mind to the heart.

The Voice as a Musical Instrument

As I mentioned earlier, people frequently say to me, "I can't find my voice!" This is a very curious statement. It's also true—in a way. Where is the voice? I can't show it to you. No matter how hard you look, you won't be able to see it.

When all these beautiful people tell me they can't "find" their voice, they're assuming they don't have one. This creates an interesting dilemma: what can they do, buy one? These people are actually expressing discontent with impediments that prevent them from developing the voice. It's easier to believe that the voice is not there than to recognize that we are actually standing in its way.

As I mentioned earlier, the voice is an instrument made of muscle and breath. It lives within our bodies of skin, muscle, bone, and blood. When we imagine the voice as a musical instrument instead of a mythical Holy Grail for which we must constantly search, it becomes something we can actually approach, work with, and refine.

Personally, I never thought of myself as a singer. This happy accident freed me from psychological considerations of any kind. To me the voice was simply an instrument—something I could learn to play and something I learned to take care of. The best part is that I didn't have to buy a heavy case to cart it around!

This is what I learned about taking care of the instrument of the voice:

It needs to be lubricated.

It needs to be toned.

It needs to be tuned.

It needs to be kept warm.

Most of all, it needs to be played.

If we work with the voice as an instrument, playing it becomes much more natural. The moment we project emotional or psychological limitations of any kind on the voice, the harder it is to play. Indeed, the voice prefers to be held as a selfless instrument. When we were children, what did we do? We played with

our voices as if they were shiny new toys with unlimited potential for joy and expression. Nothing stood in our way.

Common emotional impediments of the voice include fear
of not being perfect, of making a mistake, of failing, of being
judged, of being out of tune. Unrealistic expectations can also
be an impediment. We may desire to sing well, to perform perfectly, to be "the best"—but only by accumulating real-time
singing hours can we meet those expectations.

The voice is felt, of course, as an emotional instrument. Yet it
has nothing to do with the personal stories that might trigger inhibitions. When we gently approach our instrument as yoga, we can
release the story. The voice will then naturally fuel from, reveal,
and clear deep emotions instead of being compromised by them.

Care and Feeding of the Voice

Our vocal instrument is also part of our physical condition. Its
performance can vary depending on the rhythms of metabolism,
lung capacity, and range of motion—not to mention what is happening in our life, the weather, and if we feel hot or cold, sick or
well. The voice gets dry and tired, and it requires a lot of care.

The food we eat is very important. For example, dairy and
wheat products produce Vocal Enemy Number One: phlegm.
Casein, the naturally occurring protein in dairy products,
can promote the formation of phlegm, the thick, sticky form
of mucus that obstructs the voice. Drinking milk can make
phlegm even thicker and more irritating to the throat. Needless
to say, this is not conducive to producing our best vocal sounds,
although this is very sad for a European-raised person like
myself. So I've learned to save my bit of bread and cheese for
after a recording session, never before.

A dry throat can damage the voice over time. I'm talking about the rough, scratchy, sometimes itchy feeling in the
throat that's commonly caused when the mucous membranes
dry out—often as a result of allergies, a dry environment, air

conditioning, vocal strain, breathing through the mouth, or lack of sufficient fluids. Sugar can contribute to dehydration, so I avoid it as well.

Unlike man-made musical instruments, the voice can get tired. When we sing or talk too much, the best medicine is to rest the voice and treat it with plain hot water and honey. Lemon and honey are also a sublime remedy for a dry or achy throat. I also recommend the herbs Echinacea, goldenseal, propolis, and Angelica (for treatment of colds and flu) and Collinsonia (for smoothing and relaxing the larynx and mucous membranes). Licorice and cardamom spices are also helpful. For more information concerning natural ways to support vocal health, see the resources section at the end of the book.

Singing in a certain way—using long tones and other techniques described in this book—also helps relax and clear the voice. Follow your intuition; your voice will tell you what it likes. A serene mind and body make the best carrying case for our precious instrument.

The voice is an instrument we can polish and refine, but it requires a little bit of yoga in order to do so: two times a week for maintenance, three times a week for advancement, and five times a week for beauty. The following exercises are good for soothing the voice when it's tired or overused.

exercise 7   Soothing the Tired Voice

Try these practices, individually or in sequence, to release the free flow of the voice when your voice feels tired or strained.

1. Humming: With the lips touching slightly, exhale on a long soft hum. Try keeping as much air inside as possible when exhaling on the hum. You can change pitch, but keep it around middle range. Then, rest in silence.

2. Gentle toning: Sing a long tone on a single syllable, such as *hu* or *eh*. On the same breath, consciously shift the shape of your lips to produce a different syllable, such as *hu-ah or eh-oo*.

Afterward, fix yourself a cup of hot tea of your choice, and put plenty of honey in it. Your voice (and you) will appreciate it.

TONE AS A SPIRITUAL REALITY

Let's go back to the question of "finding" the voice. If we can't see it or touch it, does it really exist? Of course not!

I'm playing with your mind now. As voice yogis, we know that the true nature of the mind is emptiness and clarity. It is like a mirror: whatever you put there, it reflects; yet there is nothing there. The voice is like the mind: whatever quality we attribute to it is reflected in it. The true nature of the voice is energy, aiming to be expressed freely.

What is it that makes us say of a friend, "God, she really has a voice!" Do we imagine that she actually has a different instrument than we do, a golden flute, tucked away somewhere deep inside? Does she have a completely different configuration of muscles, a different source of breath? Or are we talking about the tone we hear when she sings? Yes! We love the tone. Her tone takes us to another place. Tone is energy, and we humans have the capacity to connect with energy that can be liberating.

Just for a moment, close your eyes and engage in inner listening. Imagine there is a universal tone streaming all around you and that you can link yourself with this tone, feeling it flow and resound through you. As the tone moves, both inside and outside of you, you find yourself becoming one with the universal tone.

For Rudolf Steiner, the esteemed esoteric philosopher of the early twentieth century, the experience of tone was spiritual. He affirmed that singing is not only a physical process, but one that "must be freed from a mechanical approach and the singer awakened to an understanding of true tone, to the appreciation of tone as a spiritual reality."[1]

According to Steiner, the experience of tone connects us to spiritual worlds that remind us of our source, our place of origin.[2] Tone, therefore, is spiritual energy that reflects the universal tone that streams around us. Tone exists in the etheric, or subtle, realms. "Tone is carried through the air to our ears, but it is the *etheric* which carries the real essence of the tone to our inner being," said Steiner. "An intensified listening carries the outer tone within, and the subsequent inner experience greatly affects the tone that can be sung."[3]

Steiner foresaw the possibility of a new approach to singing "wherein the singer will have the all-engrossing experience of the whole being as a 'resounding column of tone.' The entire etheric organization of the human being—all of his life forces . . . then becomes involved in the singing process. One's whole being sings."[4]

In later chapters we will see how my practice and theory of singing integrates the idea of the etheric tone developed by Rudolf Steiner and the Eastern tradition of sound and voice, giving birth to the Yoga of the Voice.

As I said earlier, yoga is a path that leads to union. When vocal technique meets yoga, the processes of breathing, phonation, articulation, and resonance are approached as one system—one experience where body, sound, and consciousness meet.

As we delve into technique, we are going to get more familiar with the different aspects that make up the "body" of the voice. These are the resonating chambers of the belly, the chest, and the head; the spine that supports them all; the precious throat; and our particular meticulous articulators: the lips, the teeth, and the tongue. The whole instrument, together with how we play it, creates the spiritual magic of tone.

5

The Body of the Voice

The voice is light itself. If the light has
become dim, it has not gone out, it is there. It
is the same with the voice. If it does not shine,
it only means that it has not been cultivated.
You must cultivate it again, and it will begin
to shine again.
HAZRAT INAYAT KHAN

Having become acquainted with the potential of our instrument, we can devote ourselves to the cultivation of tone magic by engaging our whole being. In this chapter, we focus on the body of the voice. Like all forms of yoga, the Yoga of the Voice begins with posture. Singing and the etheric tone rely on mindfulness. An attentive mind directs the body to express the full potential of the voice.

THE FOUR CORNERS OF THE FEET

The first thing to remember is that we have feet. They support and ground us, conducting energy from the earth to the heavens and helping us stand upright. Support of our breath starts with how well we support ourselves with the four corners of the feet; that stability continues up the body all the way to the head.

We begin our practice by adjusting our balance until the weight is distributed over the whole foot: toes to heel and side to side. The knees should be soft and slightly bent, and the hips should align with both the knees and ankles. Continuing our awareness upwards, the chin is parallel to the floor and the eyes are softly closed or only slightly open—free from the need to look at or take anything in. Soft eyes are aligned with soft tone.

The voice likes to be open and free, so it is happiest when the body is comfortable and calm. The hands are open and empty, the arms are relaxed, and the four corners of our feet supply the foundation for the entire body. These points of posture (as I like to call them) are used in many exercises, and they will become natural as you develop your practice. To experience this, try the practice of the Dancing Breath that follows.

exercise 8 Dancing Breath

This *qi gong* exercise brings awareness to the support of the feet and energizes your posture.

1. Bring your attention to the four corners of your feet and shift your weight from front to back and side to side until your weight is evenly distributed over the whole foot.

2. With knees slightly bent and hands hanging to your sides, open your fingers wide, making an energetic connection between the hands and feet.

3. As you inhale, softly bend the elbows. Raise your hands and forearms no higher than the chest, then let them down as you exhale. Let your hands completely relax as they flow with the motion of your arms. The arm movement reflects the movement of the breath up and down along the central axis of your body from the pelvis to the solar plexus.

4. Repeat this several times, until you feel completely comfortable with the rhythm of the breath and the body. Let your shoulders remain naturally dropped and relaxed. The torso can be still but flexible like bamboo.

THE SINGING SPINE

A flexible spine means a flexible voice. When we involve our spine in sound, we get a more refined quality of tone. We want the spine to be awakened because it is the column that our tone travels through. It's where our energy lives. When the energy travels freely up and down inside this etheric column, breath and tone naturally open the chakras. We don't need to invest much effort in "trying to open" the chakras. We are led by dharana—single-pointed attention—and by minimal movement. This will do the job.

The Vedic tradition of India plays with this same idea. By placing our focus on the subtle body as we produce sound, we become aware of *kundalini* (the energy that resides at the base of the spine, according to Vedic teachings) and the chakras (the energy centers positioned along the spine). This awareness allows us to connect directly with higher consciousness and with skillful methods to unleash the flow of energy channeled in the ethereal body's chakra system. Imbalances of all kinds form knots in the chakras that translate into physical blockages.

When we use the power of the spine to sing, we are effectively stimulating all our glands with sound. The glands are associated with the chakras—from the pineal gland, the pituitary gland, and the hypothalamus (all located in the mid-brain just above the top of the spine), and downward to the thyroid, thymus, adrenal glands, pancreas, and gonads. Traditional Chinese Medicine teaches that healthy glands make for long life, which is why many Chinese make chanting a lifelong practice. The glands represent the physical body, while the chakras represent the subtle, or etheric, body.

Singing as a yogic practice becomes a means to bridge the power of the subtle or ethereal body with activity of the physical body. As we move closer and closer to the appreciation of tone as a spiritual reality, we begin to manifest the healing power of the voice. The Singing Spine practice that follows awakens the subtle body and aligns both the physical and subtle bodies with the transformative potential of tone.

exercise 9 The Singing Spine

This practice warms up the chakras, releases their energetic flow, and enhances your affirmative connection with life force. The singing spine is a true metaphysical experience in every breath. This vocal technique is widely used to train singers and to diagnose vocal impediments.

1. Closing your lips, hum inwardly toward the spine. You are connecting to the tone within.

2. Scanning, go up and down the spine on an inward hum. Starting with a low tone from your belly, raise the pitch as you go up the spine. Usher the tone up and down the spine by moving the hands and arms up and down. If you encounter breaks or impediments in any part of your range, you can go up and down in that particular area, using your hands as if opening and closing a zipper.

Repeat softly until you perceive the whole range of your voice warming up and expanding.

3. You can repeat this whole exercise at least three times, scanning from high to low registers. Invite yourself to explore. Dwell, vibrate, move, and free any place the energy feels constrained or low.

exercise 10 Ball of Light

If you have time for only one exercise, this is the one to practice because it involves the whole body and opens the chakras along the spine. Notice how you feel before and after this practice.

1. Standing with your feet hip-distance apart, bend from the hips as far down as you can comfortably go. Keep your eyes open for this exercise.

2. Letting your body hang like a rag doll, bring the hands to the face as you inhale—as if bringing water up from a stream to wash your face. Lower the hands as you exhale, and release your upper body toward the ground, relaxed and free of any weight.

3. Still bending at the hips, place your hands as if you were lifting a large ball of light. Gently pick up this ball as you move very slowly to a vertical position. Keep your gaze on this weightless ball of light as you raise it higher, slowly bringing it above your head.

4. With shoulders dropped and eyes open, bend backward comfortably, then release the light ball as you open your voice on a long *ah*.

INWARD SINGING

A remarkable technical discovery of the Yoga of the Voice is the practice of inward singing. We're usually taught to sing out, and our attention and energy go outward with the breath. When we sing inwardly, however, we keep this vital energy and focus inside. We make a conscious choice to send the sound inward toward the spine. The sound reverberates directly against our bones, and the whole back resonates like a harp. We sing the spine to life.

Our intention to keep the sound inside creates a dynamic tension that results in a deep and clearing sound. We hear this deep tone in the singing of many indigenous and African cultures.

When we direct the air we receive from the universe inwardly, we *inspire* the spine, revitalizing those mysterious entities called chakras. They respond by giving us more power to sing. As the etheric body awakens, our whole being transforms, as Rudolf Steiner described, into "a resounding column of tone."

Singing inwardly is an improvement over what we hear too often—singers expelling most of their air at the beginning of the tone. As a result, we hear the breath more than the tone. More significantly, when we use too much air on the attack, we run out of it. Then life feels short and the tone sounds forced. Intending the tone inside results in more breath control, energy, and connection. Singing in this way makes us want to sing more and more—and that is the whole point of this book.

We can hear this kind of powerful inward singing in many legendary jazz singers, in Native American medicine chants, and among indigenous tribes of Africa, such as the whispered voices of the Burundi. The following exercise takes us imaginatively to the African savannah for an experience of this potent vocal technique. Listen closely to the audio track to become familiar with the quality of the sound and the pronunciation of the syllables.

(▶) Listen to track 6: Inward Singing

exercise 11 Inward Singing

This practice opens the back and releases the flow of the energy centers, or chakras, all along the spine.

1. In a relaxed standing position, imagine yourself in the African savannah. Feel the warm earth supporting the four corners of your feet; feel the sun on your chest.

2. Inhaling softly, fill your belly and chest with air. Keeping the air in the belly as much as possible, direct your attention toward your spine while sounding very slowly and repeating any combination of the following sounds:

hum (pronounced "hoom")

eh

awe ("ah-way")

eeya ("ee-yah")

lui ("loo-ee")

heim ("hay-eem")

mam ("maam")

ile ("ee-lay")

aye ("ah-yay")

exercise 12 Variations on Inward Singing

1. Experiment with sending different sounds to different areas of the spine and body, while invoking the spirits of nature and calling in the deities of the African grasslands.

2. Following this practice, lie on your back with your arms resting alongside your body, or stand against a wall. Let your body and mind enjoy and abide in the silence.

THE WINGS OF THE VOICE

Energy and power run along the spine—up and down, up and down. To keep the spine more flexible, we spontaneously move the arms and hands. The singing technique of the Yoga of the Voice focuses on these six key points of posture in the body: softened eyes, relaxed shoulders, the shifting shape of the lips, flexibility of the spine, the space around the navel, and how the hands move to connect with sound.

My hands taught me how to sing. I noticed that all the great singers move their hands. As a diligent observer, I perceived a direct connection between the contour and position of the fingers, which we call a *mudra,* and the way the arms move to shape and release the tone. In the Sama Vedas, a sacred Hindu text known as the Book of Song, these movements of hands and arms are called *hasta prayaogas.* They are also an integral part of the Yoga of the Voice practices.

When we sing, it is useful to imagine that we are flying. When we have to contend with flying, we realize we need wings and some support. We turn to the hands, the arms, and the elbows, knowing that we absolutely count on them to stay aloft. Yes, the elbows are most important when we sing and soar. With conscious movement of the elbows and arms, we reach the high and low notes with ease. The arms become wings. We become like the birds, the greatest singers on the planet. We sing with wings, just like the birds.

There is a delicate balance between attention and movement. The movement is always minimal—like the Italian term, *piccolo,* which means "small" and is used in musical notation. Too much movement, however, and our concentration moves around too much as well. When we move the arms and fingers subtly and naturally, like a calligraphy brush, we feel that we are delicately touching the sound. I hear myself repeating this little koan all the time: *touch what you sing and play what you sing.*

We encourage natural and organic movements of the hands, fingers, and arms that arise spontaneously from awakened consciousness, rather than a defined series of postures that could lead to rigidity. Like the hands of an orchestra conductor directing a delicate symphonic passage, these subtle movements enhance the quality of our listening, self-expression, and connection with the Beyond. You can try this with the Hands as Clouds exercise that follows.

exercise 13 Hands as Clouds

This variation of the Dancing Breath is a great exercise to balance the metabolism while also warming and strengthening the lungs and releasing any excess pressure in the diaphragm. This practice is from ancient Chinese qi gong.

1. Either sitting or standing, move your hands as if softly gathering the breath toward the center of your body, keeping the shoulders down and back, elbows low and pointing toward the earth.

2. Bring your spine and lungs into the movement by contracting the chest in a concave position as you exhale, and by expanding it in a convex position as you inhale. Enjoy the contraction and expansion of the diaphragm.

3. Do this several times for as long as the movement feels fresh and feels good.

THE BELLY

The belly is the cauldron where we warm the muscles and "cook" the breath, turning it into energy for singing—and for living. It's essential to bring the air back into the belly because this air is prana, our supply of universal life force.

As a musical instrument, our body can be compared to the Indian tamboura, a long-necked stringed instrument with a bulbous resonating chamber, like a gourd, at the base. This chamber is the biggest space on the instrument, so it produces and resonates the most sound. Our belly is where *we* have the most room. We want to warm up the air in the belly to get the best quality of the voice when we sing. Engaging the belly gives us more space to work with sound.

Muscles we use for singing are also in the belly. To naturally strengthen the base of the cauldron, it's useful to apply a very slight tension to the sphincter muscles when we breathe in and release it as we breathe out. This closes and opens the circuit of energy and helps us keep the cauldron burning, naturally creating a molecular and vital rhythm that improves all our functions, from digestion to singing a lullaby.

We want to keep the breath inside our body as much as possible when we sing. This means keeping the air in the belly, but without tension, especially in the muscles of the neck or the shoulders. By moving the warm air from the belly up and down, we recycle the energy and feel we can sing forever. Breath control and support develop effortlessly. You can practice this with the following exercise.

exercise 14 Warming the Breath

This practice warms and relaxes the belly and breath.

1. While standing, bring your attention to the belly. Inhaling, imagine bringing the breath deep into the belly.

2. Close the sphincter muscles slightly, effortlessly, with no tension.

3. As you breathe in and out, slowly bring the arms up and down to chest height with the elbows pointing down, as you did in the practice for Dancing Breath.

4. Breathe in deeply, and exhale on the sound *ah*, like a deep sigh from the belly. Feel it resonating in the whole torso. Slowly release the tension of the sphincter muscles.

5. Repeat this sequence at least three times with a long and relaxed out-breath.

6. Enjoy the freshness of the still point within, where breath and stillness meet the vibration of silence.

THE CHEST

The chest is another large resonating chamber. We can visualize it as the bellows of the voice, like the bellows of an accordion or a sruti box (one of our favorite Yoga of the Voice instruments).

This is what really happens: the intercostal muscles between our ribs assist the bellows to open and close in all directions, in and out, forward and back, side to side, and up and down. The big breath mover is the diaphragm, a dome-shaped sheet of muscle between the chest cavity and the abdomen, which is attached to the base of the sternum, the lower ribs, and the spine. The *Merck Manual* describes this process as follows:

"When the diaphragm contracts and moves lower, the chest cavity enlarges, reducing the pressure outside the lungs. To equalize the pressure, air enters the lungs. When the diaphragm relaxes and moves back up, the elasticity of the lungs and chest wall pushes air out of the lungs."[1]

The chest is very close to the belly, and they work together. We want to become very friendly with the dance of the diaphragm in the process of developing the voice. This muscle, together with the abdominal muscles, moves the breath up and down through our whole instrument. As we pay more attention to the movement of the chest, the act of breathing becomes unforced. We discover how good it feels when we are "being breathed." Rather than trying to control our breath, we can let the breath breathe us, as we do in the following exercise.

exercise 15   Happy Diaphragm

This exercise can be done sitting, lying down, or standing to bring awareness to the diaphragm and release tension.

1. Interlace your fingers and stretch your arms above your head, keeping the shoulders dropped. The insides of your elbows should face each other, and there should be no pressure on your fingers.

2. Take a long, slow stretch to one side, reaching along the side from hip to fingertips. Return to the center and do the same stretch on the other side.

3. With arms still overhead, release the fingers to hold your left wrist with your right hand. Take a long, slow stretch sideways to the right. Switch hands and stretch to the other side. Be sure to breathe in and out on each side.

4. Let your arms down, and relax for a moment. Feel the difference after the stretch.

5. Bringing your arms back overhead, look over one shoulder and rotate the spine to that side, keeping your arms aligned with your ears as much as you comfortably can. Return to center and repeat on the other side.

Each of these stretches works with a different group of muscles. Continue the practice until you feel your diaphragm smiling.

The voice that resonates in the chest is very easy and natural, giving us an effortless sense of sounding. This voice has the quality of the speech voice, and I refer to it as the *natural voice*. This chest voice lets us feel at ease with our instrument. I find that when I sing with my awareness in the chest, I access a wider range of tones and never get tired. Also, the sound that resonates in the chest is warm and tuneful—it sounds good and makes us want to sing more.

The contemporary use of the term "chest voice" often refers to a specific kind of vocal coloration or vocal timbre, pitch range, or *tessitura* (literally "texture") that is fuller and louder than the head voice or falsetto. Chest timbre can add a wonderful array of sounds to a singer's interpretive palette. We are already so familiar with our chest voice when we speak that we just have to remember to make more music with it—as I invite you to do in the following exercise.

▶ Listen to track 7: Warming the Heart

exercise 16 Warming the Heart

This practice opens and warms the chest voice.

1. Standing or sitting comfortably, bring your attention to your heart.

2. Warm your hands by rubbing your palms together until you feel the heat. Place your warm hands softly over your heart.

3. Make the sound *ere-re-re* (pronounced "ay-ray-ray-ray"), on any pitch you choose. You may change the pitch if you feel like it. Imagine that the sound expands your heart center 360 degrees around your body—and outward to infinity.

4. Do this sounding for several minutes so you can savor the connection you've made between your heart and your chest.

THE THROAT

We are approaching the most delicate part of our instrument, our precious throat. We can imagine the throat as a sacred passageway designed to carry and transform air into sound. It is made of fine porcelain: handle it with care.

Some singers think of the throat as another resonating chamber and use it too much, intending to produce a big sound there. This creates tension. Bringing more attention to the throat than to the belly and chest can damage our valuable instrument. We always want to be sure not to push any muscles in the throat too hard. Let your approach to sound be gentle. A delicate control, with the right amount of tension and release, is the key to a clear and steady tone.

The muscles we rely on for singing are the diaphragm, the abdominals, and the intercostals. These take care of all the "heavy lifting." For resonance, the chest is much bigger than the throat, so is the belly. This is why we take so much care to warm the voice slowly, with long tones and small sounds from the belly and the chest, without ever keeping the air too long in the throat. I usually address this with some simple, practical advice: be gentle with your throat; it doesn't respond well to tension. A tense throat can "cut" the voice. This can happen to anyone, even to experts like Maria Callas, one of the most renowned sopranos of all time.

Where the throat *does* play a big role is in the mystery of phonation—the physiological process whereby the energy of moving air in the vocal tract is transformed into acoustic energy within the larynx. In brief, phonation is what we *do* with the sound when it reaches the vocal apparatus. We select where to send the sound according to the outcome we want and to the tone we want to make. For instance, if I want a tone that is bright and alive, I'll choose to send the sound forward right into the cheeks, with my face in a smiling gesture to create more space in the cheeks—going for the Dizzy Gillespie effect. When expanded, the cheeks make a great stereo system.

Once again, it is our intention that directs the sound where we want it to go, according to the tone (and/or the word) we desire to express. The following practice opens the imagination to the playful possibilities of vocal placement.

exercise 17 Exploring the Cave

This practice opens the voice to many different possibilities and makes us familiar with the resonating cavities of the mouth and throat. The placement—as you move the sound up, down, and around—empowers your creative imagination.

1. Concentrate on the space inside your mouth and visualize it as a cave with the hard palate as the roof and the throat as a bridge close to water.

2. Hum a tone, sending the sound up toward your palate, nasal cavity, and cheeks.

3. Repeat on as many tones as you want.

4. Hum any simple melody that resonates in the palate and move it around inside the mouth cave, exploring all the corners.

How do the subtle differences in placement affect the tone?

THE HEAD

The head is another resonating cavity. The bones of the skull and the sinus passageways provide many cavities where we can send the tone. The term "head voice" refers to the effect achieved by singing higher notes when the tone resonates more in the small spaces of the head (the nasal and sinus cavities). The head voice has a thinner, flutier sound than the chest voice, and it's naturally energizing. It stimulates the brain and makes us feel awake and alert. As with all good medicine, we don't want to overdose, so be gentle when working with the head voice to avoid a musical headache.

I find it interesting that the Western European tradition idealizes those who have access to the highest vocal registers: sopranos. Undeniably, soprano voices can sound very beautiful. In my practice, however, I prefer to approach the head voice from an ancient, liturgical, not-for-performance angle. My intention is to evoke the discreet beauty of the voices of pre-Baroque chanting, as in the music of Hildegard von Bingen, the twelfth-century Benedictine abbess, visionary, and composer. The devotional aspect of this singing makes the production of the head voice effortless. This serene high voice emanates from a higher sense of connection to which we all have access regardless of the range of our voice. I coax my voice and the voices of my students to reach amazing highs and lows. This approach represents a more natural and integrated paradigm than the traditional approach to singing higher notes (the notes that belong to a register above the speaking range). It's also very relaxing and encouraging for the mind, the body, and the voice. I invite you to try this approach in the following practice.

(▶) Listen to track 8: The Monastic Voice

exercise 18 The Monastic Voice

This practice will give you the confidence to sing as high as you want. It is so affirmative that if music schools of any tradition were to put this in their curriculum, we would have many more healthy sopranos than unhappy, wounded singers.

It's best not to sing many notes in this exercise. Keep it simple and profound—you are singing sacred music.

1. Visualize yourself within a stone-walled monastery in northern Europe surrounded by mountains, sometime in the Middle Ages. Seated or standing with hands in prayer position, allow for continual but minimal movement of the spine. Keep it flexible.

2. With a small opening of the lips (touching, but not closed like in humming), release the sound *oo*, very long, firm, and as high as possible. Keep the sound serene, aiming the sound toward the forehead and placing the sound there. Apply no effort. Soften and drop any tension you might notice in your shoulders, or any other part of your body.

3. After dwelling for a few minutes in that sound, go up and down the scale with a simple short melody, using higher and lower notes. Most important, keep the same minimal

aperture of your lips. Let the amount of notes you sing be as minimal as the aperture of your lips. Repeat the melodies, and take a few seconds to pause in between so that you can breathe softly and relax tension anywhere in your body.

4. You might feel like using any words that come to your mind. I suggest chanting these simple Latin words as long as you can: *Sanctus Sanctus Dominus,* which can be translated as "Divine Lord of All Nations."

5. Afterward, abide in divine silence, enjoying the silence as much as the music of your lips. You are celebrating the source and "taste" of Gregorian chant.

THE LIPS

The exploration of our vocal instrument takes us finally to the lips, the most visible part of the whole singing apparatus and a major player in the kinesthetic art of vocal articulation. Articulation involves using the lips and the tongue with the maximum possibility of geometric awareness—what I call the "dancing lips," which are good company for the singing spine. We move both the lips and the tongue very consciously, always remembering that they define the quality of the tone we produce.

When people inquire about the key to vocal technique, I tell them that, besides breathing correctly, it is our attention to how we move and shape the lips according to the tones or words to be produced. This is called *embouchure*—meaning the shaping of the lips to form a sound. Awareness and control of the embouchure gives power and clarity to the music of our voice, and it is the foundation for harmonic overtone chanting (the singing of two or more notes at the same time).

In his account of the nature of tone production, Rudolf Steiner tells us that the middle of the lower lip is the physical space where the inner tone meets the outer tone, the birthplace of the etheric quality of tone. On a metaphysical level, this substantiates the healing power of toning, a favorite practice for most sound healers.[2]

The articulation of the lips works in conjunction with the tongue, the teeth, and more than a hundred muscles around the mouth and in the face. When we open our lips to make the top part of our teeth visible, we notice that it is easier to produce any tone and any word. A soft smile works well, and it will make you feel good too. People will follow and smile back at you!

Vowels and consonants are both produced on the lips *sulle labbra,* as the Italians say. This is a very important piece of vocal technique—understanding that the words we are singing are composed of syllables, or phonemes, made of consonants and vowels. We penetrate into the body of tone with the consonant, while the vowel is the receptive container that we can sculpt and adorn. We want to be mindful of the open space for the vowel, embodying it, indulging in it, and making it very fluid. Right there, in the open space of the vowel, is engendered a great deal of the power of the singing voice.

exercise 19 Dancing Lips

This is a fundamental practice for improving vocal articulation and phonation. In this exercise, the sound comes from the shifting shape of the lips and does not touch the throat. You're still waking up the voice, so the sound is very gentle. If you find your hands wanting to accompany the sound, you are in a good place.

1. With your lips touching each other and a subtle placement of your tongue on the palate, hum on a relaxed long tone (any pitch or sound).

2. Experiment with degrees of pressure and forward placement of the closed lips. It's like kissing, and the vibration is as tasty as eating a ripe mango on the beach.

3. Still humming, place your awareness on the middle of the lower lip and imagine the meeting here of the outer tone with the inner *etheric* tone.

4. Open your lips, relax your jaw, and release on the sound of *ah*. With a single breath, play with intervals—the distance between any two notes. Enjoy the focused playfulness of the minimal movement of your lips, and notice how the sound of *ah* changes as you change the embouchure.

▶ Listen to track 9: Afro-Brazilian Chant: Focus on Articulation

exercise 20 Afro-Brazilian Chant: Focus on Articulation

One wonderful way to practice articulation is to sing the following prayer for Omolu (the Orishá of healing) and other chants from the Afro-Brazilian tradition. You can follow the pronunciations on the audio.

> *Orixá Oo, Orixá*
> *Orixá Oo, Orixá*
> *Ago, Ago, Meshe*
> *Orixá Le Le, Orum*

Loosely translated as "Orishá, I stand knocking at the door, Orishá, whose home is in the domain of heaven"

6

In the Beginning,
There Was Nothing but Nada

By the knowledge of sound, man obtains the
knowledge of creation . . . This knowledge acts
as wings for a man; it helps him rise from earth
to heaven, and he can penetrate through life seen
and unseen . . . He who knows the secret of the
sounds knows the mystery of the whole universe.
HAZRAT INAYAT KHAN, *The Mysticism of Sound and Music*

With the wings of the voice opened wide, we keep flying high. After a session of the Yoga of the Voice, I sometimes
invite people to talk about what they feel. I always smile when
I remember the words of one of my students who exclaimed,
"Fly Silvia!" as if promoting an airline.

I have been teaching all over the world for more than thirty
years. Wherever I go, I'm greeted by new, eager faces, and I also
encounter many others that I've seen again and again over the
years—often decades. I've always wondered, "Why do these
people keep coming back? What are they seeking? What is it

they are longing for?" It seemed a mystery to me that people keep coming together week after week, year after year, to sing with me in languages they don't even know—the way we do at our Vox Mundi schools.

In the course of writing this book, I finally understood. The answer lies in the *longing*—for a mystic connection, for spontaneity in expression, for an innocent approach to what is unknown, and to express the sound of our pure nature. Is there a better reason for us to get together to sing?

I invite you to dive with me into the mystery of sound from the very Source and to connect with sound and music not just as a musician, but as a mystic. Let's sip for a moment the heavenly wine of the Sufi poet Jalal ad-Din Rumi and see how profoundly close encounters with vibration can quench the thirst of that divine longing. Here's the poem translated by Coleman Barks.

> *The wine we really drink is our own blood . . .*
> *We give everything for a glass of this.*
> *We give our minds for a sip.*[1]

Wine is a common metaphor used by Rumi and other Sufi poets. It refers to an overwhelming ecstatic state in which we are conscious of neither our physical nor mental existence. Drinking the heavenly wine encourages us to get closer to God.

SOUND: THE CREATOR

The most ancient cultures on the planet believed that material reality is the manifestation of primordial vibration. Even the Bible teaches that "In the beginning was the Word, and the Word was with God, and the Word was God." (John 1.1)

Early and contemporary spiritual traditions, and shamans and scientists alike propose that vibration (the first sound) is the beginning of all creation. The ancient Bön and Dzogchen teachings, which predate Buddhism in Tibet, also state that sound is in the basis of all manifestation. In a newsletter of the International Dzogchen Community, Costantino Albini writes:

> In the most ancient Tibetan mythological cycles, sound is considered to be the original source of all existence. Sound, which from the beginning of time has vibrated in ineffable emptiness, arises through mutations of light and then differentiates into rays of various colors from which the material elements that make up the entire universe originate.[2]

Albini is describing how sound gives birth to light, and how light shines out in rays that become the elements—quite literally the physical matter of the universe. In many ancient traditions, sound and vibration are present as a gateway to contemplation, divination, and spiritual development. In the Vedic tradition, derived from texts originating in ancient India, the "Word," as it is conceived of in the Western Bible, is called the Nada Brahma.

The primordial and transcendent sound is considered the seed from which all of creation evolved. This is the Nada Brahma. *Nada,* or vibration, is the first audible sound, the primordial roaring, the resounding flow that heralds the beginning of the evolutionary process from which energy and matter radiate. Brahma, the creator God, is the creative power that animates one's divine consciousness with the power to move the heart.

The original, eternal Nada vibrates at the highest rate of frequency. In physics, when an object vibrates at an inconceivable speed it appears to the eye that it's not moving. It's fascinating that the highest point of vibration is stillness; in the dimension of sound, this is experienced as silence. Above a certain level of high frequency, sound becomes inaudible and can only be perceived subjectively. The ears cannot perceive sounds that are vibrating at such a high rate. Thus, Nada is both the beginning

of all sounds and manifestations, and, in the realm of consciousness, Nada is the vibratory rate of silence.

I've always thought it an amusing paradox that *nada*
in Spanish (and Portuguese, for that matter) means "nothing," while the same word in Sanskrit relates to "everything."
Whatever way you look at it, an experience of Nada—savored
in the intimate union of sound and silence—becomes the super-
highway to the Divine. I consider Nada the beginning of the
evolving poetics of sound.

OUTER, INNER, AND SECRET SOUND

According to Dzogchen, considered one of the highest teachings
of Tibetan Buddhism, there are three ways to experience sound:

1. Outer sound is physical; we *hear* it with our ears and we
    produce it with our bodies.

2. Inner sound is energetic; we *feel* it on the energetic plane
    as an opening in the chakras or as inward expansiveness.

3. Secret sound just *is;* we *perceive* it with a mind that's
    clear. It arises as a result of states of meditation. It's like a
    revelation that comes from a non-conceptual state.

Sound comes from emptiness and dissolves into emptiness
(space). The experience with sound in these three dimensions
offers us a way of harmonizing our energy at a deep level. I find
an immense transformative value in this tri-dimensional experience of sound. It makes of us total "listeners."

Sound is the seed for transformation; when sound is
expressed by a voice that integrates the breath, the body, and
the mind in instant presence, we begin to perceive the luminous
nature of the mind and the radiance of the spirit. When we
sing in this conscious way, we become sensitive to the outer

voice, the inner voice, and the secret voice. We also discover the healing energy within the voice, and the great longing is soothed. This aligns with Rudolf Steiner's concept of tone as a spiritual reality and his fascination with what he described as inner, outer, and universal tone.

I think it's the yearning for Nada that compels people to come together to sing. When we sing together, we don't have to go to the mountaintop dressed in skins and feathers and spend weeks fasting. We get to the place of inner serenity every few minutes. At the end of every long note, we have a taste of Nada. In the conscious dance of sound and silence, we always land in the nectar of Nada, where sound is silence and silence is sound. Simply delicious art!

Nada Yoga: Voice as Energy

Through music one can transcend into the mysterious sphere of silence, through time-bound rhythm cycles to timelessness, through sound space to sacred space. Music is therefore called Nada-yoga, a union of body and Spirit through vibrations.
RADHIKA SRINIVASAN, *Sacred Space*

Nada Yoga is the spiritual science of sound that originated in India around 200 BC. It is the practice of deepening consciousness through sound. We become familiar with the invisible and formless beauty of chanting sacred sound. It's a skillful means by which to develop the connection with sound as vibration, vibration as energy, and energy as life force, or prana. In Nada Yoga, words are not fixed in meaning—just sound.

Nada Yoga practices are like meditation through sound. The source of the sound may be external or internal, obvious or subtle. But the mind is focused only in the dimension of sound, becoming free from feelings, thoughts, and wanting. This is the best use for that space we call the mind. By cultivating familiarity with the mind through sound unattached to meaning, we become calmer and clearer, and the secret frequencies of wisdom can be heard.

So how does all this work in our daily practice? Through Nada Yoga, we use specific sounds to stimulate dormant currents of energy in our body-mind, and we lead our consciousness to the heart of deep love and devotion—sounds like *Om*, which represents the total vibratory nature of the universe. According to ethnomusicologist Lewis Rowell:

> The syllable *Om* . . . has been interpreted as
> the eternal syllable that contains in itself the
> entire phenomenal universe, and as a nucleus
> from which all audible sounds proceed and to
> which all such sounds must ultimately return.
> . . .The utterance of the sacred syllable is, then,
> at once, an invocation to the gods, a salutation
> to the structure of the created universe, an
> aid to meditation, a protection against error,
> a hymn of praise to life in all its forms and
> manifestations, and a symbol of integration
> and completeness.[3]

In the right circumstance, when we chant *Om*, or any sacred sound, all the cells in our body—especially our brain cells—start vibrating. When the body is vibrating while the mind is chanting, we experience harmony between the two. The body and mind fall in tune. And "I"—the "I" that is neither body nor mind—can be at peace because it is no longer being pulled in one direction by the body and in another by the mind. I like to call this an experience of soundness, a sonorous remembrance of wholeness.

According to Osho, the Indian mystic and spiritual teacher, while the body and mind are absorbed in chanting, the other "I" can slip out and become a witness. Watching from the outside, we experience amazing tranquility. We watch our body sway-ing and our mind feeling calm and quiet. We are at once the being who experiences utter peace *and* the neutral observer who stands outside the body and witnesses this phenomenon. We are in "ecstasy" (which literally comes from the Greek verb meaning "to stand out").[4]

I adore this ecstasy. In my experience, Nada Yoga is the fast track to cosmic consciousness, a selfless and illuminating state of interconnectedness with the web of life. I see Nada Yoga as the foundation of devotional chanting and all forms of healing with sound. And everybody loves it because it is intrinsically reward-ing. You don't need to be a musician to practice Nada Yoga. You just need to be a yogic practitioner or a seeker of silence.

Nada Yoga practices are about exploring sacred states of consciousness through contemplative sound. There is a sense of being in a space that is bigger than we are. In the exercises, including the Silent Om practice that follows, let the body be still, the eyes soft, and the breath calm and expansive and long, very loooooong.

exercise 21   Silent Om

This is a good practice for getting acquainted with the realm of inner and outer sound. Try this one at night to help you sleep if you're feeling agitated.

1. Sit comfortably with your back straight and eyes softly closed. Silently repeat the sound of *Om* for several minutes.

2. Next, focus on your spine and visualize a blue light ascending through the energy centers of your etheric body.

3. Try this exercise again, this time vocalizing the sound of *Om*. To connect with inner sound, be equally generous

with the vowel "o" and the articulation of the consonant "mmmm."

Does it feel any different when you vocalize the sound? What are you listening to when you are not chanting?

THE UNSTRUCK SOUND

> *Nada (vibration) is the reflective*
> *awareness of the energy of transcendental*
> *consciousness which, becoming conscious*
> *of itself, assumes the form of the unstruck*
> *sound or anahata dhwani.*
>
> from the *Netra Tantra*

The purpose of Nada Yoga is to lead the mind to discover the ultimate inner sound and the secret sound current of one's divine essence. To realize that *we* are not just our body or our mind, but our nature is the state of instant presence and awakening. Through Nada Yoga practices we can discover our true nature and explore the frequencies of our own soundness.

To connect with this inner current of sound, we can begin with audible or external sounds—of music playing or of our own voice audibly breathing or toning, for example—and gradually shift our attention to the silence after the sounds are made. Another way to connect is to play a singing bowl and follow the ringing frequency until it completely fades. We can also meet our breath and listen to the space in between our inhaling and exhaling. Or we can lead our active mind to imagine how the sound of emptiness would sound.

This transports us gently through deeper states of consciousness as we merge with the "unstruck" sound, or the *anahata nada,* the sound that is not generated by an external strike or hit, but the inner sound that is heard in deep meditation. It has a leading quality. It leads the practitioner toward the state of soundless sound—the silence within, where we connect with the primordial energy that is the Source of all that is.

Lokesh Chandra, a contemporary scholar of Buddhism and Indian art, explains the location of this transcendental sound: "The unstruck sound, anahata nada, is heard in the anahata-chakra, the psycho-energetic center located at the heart, the seat of transcendental Consciousness. In this secret seat of the Divine can be heard the immortal sound not produced by anything."[5]

In seeking a deeper understanding of the nature of unstruck sound, you may find that this next practice illuminates it for you.

exercise 22 Unstruck Sound

This is a variation of one of the most ancient exercises of Nada Yoga. It is a sonic meditation inspired by contemporary American composer Pauline Oliveros and her deep-listening sound medicine.[6]

1. Hold your hands over your eyes and plug your ears. Push gently to the point where you don't see or hear a thing from the outside. Relax your arms and your shoulders.

2. Focus your attention on internal sound. Become aware of what the sound may resemble—for example, a distant ocean, the thrum of a hummingbird, a rumble of thunder.

3. Focus your mind on the sound and keep listening to it. When the sound becomes completely clear and distinct, notice if you can hear another sound in the distant background.

4. If so, give up the first sound and follow the second sound until that becomes prominent. Then return to the first sound.

5. You can continue this process until your consciousness is only aware of listening. If any thought arises, listen to it as a sound and let it spontaneously dissolve.

Can you describe the sound you heard inside? How does your mind feel after this practice? Do you "have" a mind?

Some scholars like the term *anahad nada* better to describe the unstruck sound. Anahad implies "unlimited" sound or "sound on which no boundaries can be set," suggesting freedom and liberation of the spirit from its earthly bondage.

Whichever definition you prefer, the yogic traditions affirm that those who hear that inner vibration and meditate on it are relieved from the burden of worries, sorrows, fears, and diseases. The spirit is freed from the captivity of the senses and the physical body; consciousness becomes free from all limitations of the mind.

The awareness of the unstruck sound is a powerful, evolving practice that takes us directly to pure love. Once again, the only requirement is to cultivate familiarity with the practice and where the practice leads us. Many people report a sensation of being "cleansed" from within when doing these exercises. Always remember that sound clears thought and purifies the mind.

The following practice allows you to deepen your experience of the unstruck sound. As you do the exercise, keep in mind that there is no right or wrong; the point is in the exploration and discovery.

exercise 23 Sounding the Sound Within

This practice helps clear the mind and release excess energy.

1. Repeat the Unstruck Sound practice.

2. When an inner sound becomes clear and prominent, see if you can make the sound audible with your voice.

3. After a couple of minutes, clear and slowly dissolve the sound you've intoned by taking a deep breath.

4. Rest in the silence you just created. Notice how you feel inside and outside. Abide in the silence.

RESONANCE OF A SPIRITUAL KIND

> *Every breath you take contains an atom*
> *breathed out by Marilyn Monroe.*
> MARCUS CHOWN, *Quantum Theory Cannot Hurt You*

The experience of Nada allows for the awakening of life to life, of silence to sound, and sound to silence. There is a secret call for resonance within the emotional life of a molecule. In the pulse of a lonely atom, the naked spirit of creation is revealed. In the first breath of *Om* the whole universe of sound is revealed.

The longing of the musician is the longing for more Nada. Nada is the practice of resonance with one's inner silence. The search in the longing seems to be the primordial "exciting" impulse to create art, music, and the art of living.

Resonance involves transferring energy between two or more systems, humans, or sounds. The experience is so engaging. This suggests to me that human resonance is the essential force behind longing. Longing for resonance amplifies our desire to re-sound with and to sing with. We long to be in resonance with all that we long for, and nothing is more available to guide our way than singing. Through chant, we open like a flower. We *are* the flower.

There is a longing for resonance at the beginning and end of a chant, musical epic, or symphonic journey. There is resonance of this kind in every breath and every *Om*—in every prayer, every hope, every love story that ends with a kiss.

▶ Listen to track 10: Unbroken Sound

exercise 24 Unbroken Sound

This practice is for tuning our energy and voice with the changing light of the universe. It is especially powerful when practiced before dawn. Cosmic consciousness becomes a felt experience through sound. For this exercise, it's useful to have a recording of a drone playing in the background. You may, of course, use the drone on audio track 2.

1. Meet with your breath and tune your voice to the drone, if you are using one. Softly and slowly intone the following syllables: *sa – ah – naa – ree – na – om* (pronounced "sah-ah-naah-ree-nah-omm").

2. Sing all the syllables in sequence on the same note, using one long breath. Focus your attention on making one long unbroken sound and on slowly spacing out the syllables to fill one breath.

3. Keeping the tone long and smooth, pay attention to how much you can lengthen each syllable—with minimal microtonal modulation in one long breath.

4. Notice the slight shifts of your lips, vocal cavity, and tongue while articulating the consonants distinctly.

5. Repeat for several minutes, taking rests between each breath.

6. Practice chanting the sounds more slowly each time.

Sound: The Transformer

Why are these sound practices so powerful? It's something about bringing breath, mind, sound, and consciousness together before entering into the dimension of song. They collectively take us to a transpersonal zone of existence where our attention becomes very inclusive and very spacious. We are in the space of divine love—no longer in the realm of "me, me, me, I am doing this," but part of something much larger and less personal.

The practices of Nada Yoga are especially good for people who have trouble relaxing or sleeping—the practices put them in the "zone." For people with physical pain or ongoing physical difficulties, opening the voice with Nada Yoga allows them to detour from the pain and move toward a lighter and more sustaining transpersonal dimension.

Sound travels through consciousness and has the power to transform everyday occurrences into a spiritual dimension through qualities of tone, rhythm, and vocal expression. A simple example of this is the piercing tone produced by ringing Tibetan bells or cymbals, which generates highly acute harmonics that permeate the mind with a sense of transcendence leading to silence and serenity.

Every spiritual tradition of the world uses sound to facilitate the passage between states of consciousness. As we enter the inspiring realm of Nada by intoning sacred seed syllables and invocations, we tap into deeper and more luminous realms of appreciation. Nada Yoga practices reconnect us with the energy of the central channel, where our spine and the chakras abide, activating the relationship between subtle levels of consciousness and the spirit world.

Many Nada Yoga practices are shamanic in nature due to their transformative and spiritual quality. You may discover this by chanting the words "Ananda Hari Om" in the exercise that follows. The Indian mystic and teacher Osho writes of these sounds:

The significance of these mystic sounds goes far higher than its meaning, and the power is in the very sound. Ananda Hari Om enters in the heart and resounds within your whole being, creating a subtle harmony, a deep peace, a strange feeling of fulfillment, of being at ease with the world, with the universe, with existence itself.[7]

(▶) Listen to track 11: Ananda Hari Om

exercise 25   Ananda Hari Om

Repeating this mantra is like the loving embrace of a big, warm mama: protection at its sweetest. It is a prayer to unite consciousness with the bliss of divinity. *Ananda* means "bliss," and *hari* refers to "divinity."

1. Using the audio download, I invite you to chant along with the mantra Ananda Hari Om—slowly and with relaxation. Dwell in each syllable, with very minimal and slow micromodulations of the tone up and down.

2. "Dissect" each of the sounds and syllables in the mantra to discover its essential resonance with consciousness, magic, mood, and power.

SHABDA YOGA: YOGA OF THE WORD

Meaningful words introduce us to the realm of Shabda Yoga. In Sanskrit, *shabda* means "sound, speech, or utterance" in the sense of linguistic performance. Whereas Nada Yoga focuses on sound, pure vibration, and non-lexical syllables, Shabda Yoga connects sound to the realm of language and meaning.

Shabda Yoga is the yoga of the inspired word, specifically the practice of chanting seed syllables and mantras. These sacred sounds transmit to us the transformational power of their lineage and help activate the brain, the body, and the heart. They also serve to protect our mind from any spiritual harm.

In the Hindu tradition, the very beginnings of language are represented by what we call *bija,* or seed syllables. Seed syllables are a combination of vowels and consonants. As ancient sound formulas that have come from unbroken traditions through the ages, bija syllables are super-charged with spiritual information. Each sound in the Sanskrit language is a seed syllable, which is one reason the Vedic mantras (composed of seed syllables) are so potent.

Seed syllables are like sound parents. They represent the moment of conception of divine energy and power—the merging of male and female, solar and lunar. The vowels are female, receptive and illuminative, bringing light and radiance to the mind and consciousness. The male qualities of action and penetration are in the consonants. For maximum benefit, when we chant these sounds we want to be aware of giving the same attention and duration to the vowel and to the consonant—the female and male merging in unity. In every *hum, aum,* or *Om,* remember that sound and consciousness are making love. You may get the feel of this seminal unity by doing the following exercise.

▷ Listen to track 12: Brahm, the Creator

exercise 26   Brahm, the Creator

Brahm emanates from Shabda-Brahma, the Word that is God, the Beginningless and Endless God, from which the unfolding of the universe commences. With repetition and familiarity, this seed sound connects us with the Source of all creation, providing an inner sense of creativity and inspiration.

1. Sit comfortably, and with both your right and left hands form a mudra by joining the thumb in a circle with the index finger.

2. Repeat the syllable Brahm (the vowel is pronounced "ah") with long tones, feeling the vibration of the ending *mmm* sound resonating in the forehead.

3. Intone the syllable as long and continuously as you can, in the most relaxed way possible. Practice slowly, letting your energy flow with a gentle movement of breath, keeping your arms and hands in mudra gesture.

Bija: Planting the Seed

Each seed syllable is pregnant with the energy of a deity from which it manifests and into which it dissolves, with the power to evoke a particular quality, such as compassion, healing, or clarity. By sounding the syllable we bring the quality of the deity into felt experience, supporting the process of opening and the free flow of energy.

These ancient seed sounds open the mind to a deeper receptivity. Chanting these sounds purifies thoughts and transforms emotions. The mind clears. The body feels. The voice is the conduit.

You don't have to be a musician to master the beauty of intoning these essential sounds. I suggest a dose of Bija Syllables every morning and another before you go to sleep. The practice, below, just might change your mind—and life—forever.

Listen to track 13: Bija Syllables

exercise 27 Bija Syllables

Each of these single syllable sounds connect you with a deity and her divine qualities through sounding and toning.

As you slowly chant the seed sound, connect your breath with sound and sound with your body. Allow for deep resonance with the effortless tone of your voice, chanting the syllable again and again. Let the sound and breath be long.

Aim (pronounced "ah-eem"), seed syllable of Saraswati, goddess of knowledge, music, and the arts

Hrim ("hreem"), seed syllable of Shakti, the divine mother

Krim ("kreem"), seed syllable of Kali, goddess of energy and transformation

Shrim ("shreem") seed syllable of Lakshmi, goddess of prosperity and generosity

VOICE AS THE BREATH OF GOD

> *The Function of Music . . . is to quiet the mind to make it more sensitive to Divine intervention.*
> from the *Sama Vedas*

When sound comes from our own voice, the power of musical vibration intensifies in our body. The experience of breathing deeply, dwelling in one note, feeling tone revitalizing the body, blending our own voice with other voices in essential unison, is deeply inspiring, offering rare glimpses of the sacred Source. It's exhilarating. We experience God as a fierce impulse to love, to listen, and to keep singing. Sound becomes divine healing.

Voice sings
Breath shapes sound
Mind mirrors the breath of God

God breathes us
Sound becomes light
Joy abounds
Word dissolves in Nada
Everything becomes nothing
We . . . are All

Soham

7

The Yoga of the Voice
FROM BREATH TO CHANT

Real music is not for wealth, not for honors
. . . it is one kind of yoga, a path for realization
and salvation to purify your mind and heart
and give you longevity.
ALI AKBAR KHAN

Chapter 6 introduced us to the destination of Nada Yoga—of ultimate transpersonal connection through sound—the space of: *who is singing?* The question is, how do we get there? What path is going to take us to that place of liberation through sound? What's the vehicle that will take us to Nada?

This chapter is about getting there—the program that will allow us to accomplish what we want to experience with sound, step by step. We're coming to the essence of the Yoga of the Voice—the operating system that allows us to systematically connect the awakening vibrations of our voice with the crystal-clear emptiness of the mind.

YOV Operating System

Installation of this software is simple and minimal. Because of its simplicity, we can easily apply it and embody it as our practice. But first we need to return to *dharana*—the flashlight beam of single-pointed attention. In the Yoga of the Voice program, one practice relies on the other. All are interrelated. So the focus of our attention determines how fruitfully we move forward in our practice, not to mention our life. How we pay attention to the breath affects our capacity to open to sound, which influences the quality of our tone, and so on.

These are the basic components of the Yoga of the Voice program:

Breath

Sound

Tone

Seed Syllables

Invocation

Vocal Meditation

Mantra

Prayer

Chant

Using these elements, we move sequentially from one to the next, with our attention completely focused on our experience within each. Dwelling in the infinite potential of each component, we begin to discover that the boundaries between one and another are permeable. Once we become comfortable with the *form,* the order becomes *flow.* We need the form, the yoga, so that we can be very free within it. As we cultivate familiarity with our practice, it becomes a seamless flow from breath to chant.

The practice begins before you even notice—in the moment of stillness before you start. Then, to truly feel free, you need to follow the form first. When the form becomes embodied, you'll discover that you are never alone while practicing—you are channeling a higher force that guides you. Whether you call it lineage, the teacher, or the Divine, you'll notice the invisible company, because there is no more tension.

Everything that follows in this chapter refers to this form. You can always come back here when you are lost or when you need to reboot.

READ ME FIRST!

This is the Read Me document. You'll want to read this to find out how to "install the software" and sign the "terms and agreements" of the Yoga of the Voice.

You can think of the following as the interface between sound and states of consciousness. It is a way to experience each component, while exploring dimensions of the voice.

1. Setting Intention—We set our intention to free the voice from personal constraints or pre-conditioning and to benefit all beings by means of the practice of singing. The intention we set is incremental; as we develop, we refine and expand our intention in order for the practice to evolve.

2. Connecting—As we engage with each component of the practice (breath, tone, seed syllables, etc.), we bring our focus solely to the dimension of sound. There is nothing but awareness of sound.

3. Dwelling—Abiding in one sound enables us to enhance and align our auditory perception. By dwelling (with drones, long breaths, and long tones), we evoke a feeling of spaciousness—physically, psychically, and vocally—that encourages us to dwell even deeper.

4. Vibrating—Slowly, our senses start playing the invisible strings of our ethereal body. The focus is on vibration; as it begins to permeate our physical and emotional bodies, we start to feel "sense"-ational.

5. Moving—As we become one with the stream of sound, it moves naturally up and down and around, slithering slowly like a snake through the spine, and awakening our entire mind-body-spirit system.

6. Transforming—An alchemical process has taken place. Settling into deep silence, we perceive that our energy, our state of being, and our consciousness have shifted. Mind and body are clear, and tensions have melted as a natural sense of joy unveils. We are not the same person we were when we began.

We engage with each of the components of the Yoga of the Voice—breath, sound, tone, seed syllables, invocation, vocal meditation, mantra, prayer, and chant—and we move through this same form always—intending, connecting, dwelling, vibrating, moving, and transforming.

Congratulations! You have successfully installed the Yoga of the Voice operating system.

BREATH

Breath is where the voice lives. Without breath, there is no Yoga of the Voice because our attention to breath determines how we sing. All sonorous yogic practices involve the movement of breath—where breath becomes sound—and the mind, through breath, follows sound. Breath, quite simply, is the Movement of Life. The breath is our built-in Wi-Fi—it connects us and takes us wherever we want to navigate.

With more awareness in the dimension of breath, the more energy we have when we sing. On a physical level, engaging and deepening our breath oxygenates the blood, activates the calming influence of the parasympathetic nervous system (our rest-and-digest response), and tones the muscles of the rib cage and abdomen, especially the diaphragm.

With our breath, we give and we receive life. The singing breath is not just concerned with how we exhale, but with the quality of the inhalation as well. We want to become very conscious of the way we bring breath into the body, because this precious breath will become the life of a tone. Then we can allow ourselves to attend to the identity of the exhalation, which comes out as music.

Breath is the sun within us, the life force. With each attentive breath, the sun warms up our heart and the energy that flows up and down the spine. The breath is the invisible bridge between our physical and subtle bodies. In the Vedic tradition, as noted earlier, the awareness of breath as life force is called prana; the Tibetans call it *lung*, or wind; in the Yoruba culture it is known as *ashé*, the dynamic force of existence that expresses itself in the air. The Chinese call it *chi*; it is known as *ki* in Japan. In the Hawaiian Kahuna tradition, this life force is known simply as the *ha*—the breath of life—from which we get the word "aloha." Our affirmative relationship with this dynamic and pervasive vibration of life is what keeps us happy, healthy, passionate, and alive.

We can constantly renew our relationship with breath through sound and movement. The result is improved well-being and a more integrated Self. When we engage with the movement of breath, we connect with ashé, with prana, with chi, with ha, with the energy of the sun and the moon. This is precisely why the healing power of sound cannot be purchased on a CD—it is about us, in real time, connecting with life.

When I was a child, I loved to play with the sounds of my breath before I fell asleep. In my child consciousness, I knew I was interacting with God. From the very beginning, I believed that breath was a way to talk to God. I recognized that some divine entity was listening to me through my breath and that every breath I took was an act of love.

As the carrier of tone, breath is the mediator between consciousness and sound. This is an important aspect of the relationship between singing and breath. As this relationship evolves, the more refined and beautiful our voice will be. All the practices we offer to free the voice rely on our conscious attention to breath. Breath is the portal, the voice is the carriage, and *you* take the journey.

exercise 28 Aware Breathing Practices

Always enter gently into your practice by aligning your posture—connecting to the earth through the four corners of the feet or the sitting bones, spine relaxed and upright, chin parallel to the floor, eyes soft. Take the time to set your intention.

1. Tapping: Energize your breath by tapping, slapping, rubbing the body, shampooing the head, and massaging the whole face and feet.

2. Pranayama: Connect with your breath by slowly inhaling for four counts, holding for three, and exhaling on eight. Keeping your eyes softly open, repeat several times.

▶ Listen to track 14: Sopro

3. Sopro: Inhale the healing power of nature and hold the breath for a few seconds, then release on a strong

exhalation that sounds like "shoo." I call this practice *sopro,*which in Portuguese means "blow." It's a chance to blow away any thoughts or feelings that may be disturbing you. This practice is used by the shamans in South America to connect with the spirit world, and also to cleanse the shaman's body from any pain or intrusion caused by the healing work. Do this practice a minimum of three times, until you feel your mind become "windy."

exercise 29 Long Straw

This practice assists our awareness of how we bring air and breath into the body and peace in the mind.

1. Sitting comfortably, feel a sense of sustained and grounded support, and become aware of your body as a musical space. Connect with your natural breathing cycle.

2. With your lips almost closed, extend the breath and exhale very long, as if breathing through a long straw. Blow very gently, slowly and evenly, sending your breath through the straw all the way to a far wall or a distant viewpoint, if you are outdoors. Do this several times, feeling your connection with space as the breath enters and leaves the body.

3. In silence, enjoy the serenity of your deeper mind.

SOUND

We are ready to move into the realm of sound and sounding. As we discussed in the previous chapter, sound is in the beginning of all creation. It is said that the primordial sound of *Om* gives birth to all manifestations. This is why sound so easily evokes our affirmative connection with nature and the elements. Sounding is a way to say "aloha" to life.

Everything in us and around us is in motion and has sound—some we can hear and some we can't. But the vibration is everywhere. Produced and transmitted by the vibration of matter at the molecular level, sound is a phenomenon that is both objective and measurable. The transmission of vibratory motion is directly proportional to the degree of perception in the auditory centers in the brain after resonating in the ear, the skin, and the bones.

It is through sound and movement that the voice communicates. As the voice is directly connected to our physical being and our energetic disposition, the simple act of making sound is a good daily workout for both the physical and the subtle body.

The practice of sounding has no rules—at this stage, we are not approaching sound from a musical perspective. Sound can be any texture, shape, or quality. In exploring pure sound, we are not restricted by considerations of tone, melody, rhythm, or any other component traditionally associated with making music. We are exploring the human capacity for expressing sounds, revisiting the threshold of what is possible. It is utterly freeing—like a baby's first discovery of all the juicy, squishy, spluttery, blowy, bellowing sounds she can make with this wonderful instrument.

Let me suggest two possible avenues as you approach the territory of sounding: the contemplative and the expressive. These two avenues are great points of entry for practice. The one you choose will depend on your individual needs and desires in the moment.

Suppose, for instance, that on one particular day, you are feeling a bit pensive or melancholic. You may not want to go wild in your approach to sound, even though in an earlier practice you felt great pulling out all the stops with the Open Sound exercise (on page 8). You may wish instead to choose practices that are more contemplative in nature, entering slowly and suiting the practice to a softer mood. On another day, you may feel like indulging the expressive quality of your voice, connecting with more variety and more vigorous sound. The objective is not to force yourself to have a particular experience, but rather to honor how you feel and connect with our authentic voice at all times. Remember the motto of the Three Fs: First feel free!

Any sound is a good sound. Our objective in connecting with sound is to let go of limitations, restrictions, inhibitions, and anything that stands in the way of playing with the symphony of sounds within and around us. When we do this, we experience how the simple phenomenon of sounding clears and opens. Sound clears everything, even sound.

The following practices serve as a reminder of the core qualities of the Yoga of the Voice: intending, connecting, vibrating, dwelling, moving, transforming. We want to stay attentive to these principles with every exercise we include in our practice.

exercise 30   Open Sound/Any Sound Revisited

This practice (from chapter 1) releases tension and fatigue, relaxes tired muscles, restores energy, and refreshes your mind. It works particularly well with children—I actually learned it from them.

1. Stand comfortably with your weight balanced on both your feet. The intention is to open to sound.

2. Connecting: Tune into your body and release the first sound that wants to come out. It might be a sigh, a soft groan, or even a vocal explosion of sound. Let whatever sound that wants to be expressed come without judgment.

3. Tune in again and let another sound out, and then another. Tune in and sound. You may find that with each

sound you release, your body finds a new starting place and the expression of sound becomes more expansive and playful.

4. Dwelling: Allow your body and voice to interact in this way for as long as you like. When you are finished, stand quietly and notice how your body and your energy feel.

5. Vibrating and Moving: Continue with a free exploration of any type of sound and see how it alters as you play with the choreography of the lips. Move your arms and legs to accompany the sound, and experiment with the different resonating cavities in your head.

You can experiment with sounds of humming, sighing, chewing, whistling, snoring, exploding sounds, puppy whines, animal calls—anything you can think of. Revisit your capacity to activate sound and release any limits you may impose on "good" or "right" or "musical" sounds.

TONE

Now that we have opened to sound, the Yoga of the Voice practice takes us over the threshold of tone. Earlier in this book, we discussed the concept of tone as a spiritual reality. Let's look at it from a different perspective: how does tone differ from sound?

To put it in the simplest terms, tone is sound in time, which adds a new dimension to our practice. Since tone lives in time, the production of tone requires attention to duration—the length of time the sound is sustained. Each tone has a specific frequency that can be measured, combined, and repeated. The specific frequency—or pitch—of the tone is what we call a "note," and it can be matched to the pitch of a piano or any other musical instrument.

Instruments I suggest for connecting with tone are tambouras, raagini boxes, harmoniums, and sruti boxes (discussed in chapter 3). With them, we play drones. Drones are particularly good to encourage listening, giving us more time to dwell in the nuances of a tone and the art of tuning. Nevertheless, whatever instrument you resonate with is good—just chanting long and short tones with your instrument of choice will trigger the magic.

What else do we need to consider for our practice? Silence. The practice of tone is also the practice of silence. Silence is the space from which sound and tone come to be, and silence is the destination to which all sounds return.

In his book *Sound and Symbol,* musicologist Victor Zuckerkandl states, "Every tone is an event. A tone contains limitless possibilities. . . . Musical tones are conveyers of forces. Hearing music means hearing an action of forces."[1]

In music, tone is like a lover—a sensual force seeking another force, another tone. In singing, tone is the color and becomes the textural quality of the voice. It's the sensibility that characterizes each voice to communicate meaning and music in a unique way. According to author and contemporary composer Dane Rudhyar, "A tone is a direct experience. . . . The experience of tone is magical in the sense that it establishes a vital mode of communication between living beings."[2]

In the beginning of creation is sound; in the beginning of singing is tone; and in the beginning of tone is toning.

▶ Listen to track 15: Toning Practice

exercise 31   Toning Practice

This practice allows for sound to follow breath and for voice to follow sound. This way of toning adjusts the nervous system, releases tension, stimulates circulation, and enhances breath power and health. It's a wonderful wellness practice—and a way to open the voice and evaluate any energetic imbalance.

1. Through a relaxed and small lip opening, release the sound of *woo*. Keeping the pitch steady, release a tone as long as your breath. Do this for several minutes.

2. While sustaining your focus on the same note, dwell in the tonal space you have created. Explore what happens to the sound when you "guide" it with minimal gestures of the hands.

3. You may continue the practice, reshaping the lip opening and alternating the pitch slightly between two neighboring notes.

4. Abide in silence and listen to the vibration *after* the sound. Notice how the length and duration of the tone relaxes all expectations and connects with both inner and outer space.

exercise 32   Toning Practice Variation:
Toning with a Drone

This toning practice is recommended for enhancing deep listening, concentration, emotional clearing, and creativity.

1. Over the subtle drone of an external instrument, such as a tamboura, sruti box, or string synthesizer patch, tone on the two-part sound *aim* ("ah-eem") through a relaxed and smiling lip opening.

2. Repeat and dwell in the tonal landscape, toning only on one or two notes, always landing back on the drone. Attune yourself to the world of unbroken toning, not yet exploring melody.

3. Keep doing this as long as it makes you happy; abide in the silence afterward.

After toning, do you notice any subtle differences in your respiration, heart rate, or quality of mind?

SEED SYLLABLES

Seed syllables introduce another aspect of the Yoga of the Voice program. Where the practice of sound connects to the element of space, and the exploration of tone leads to the awareness of time in space, seed syllables are points of entry to link with our energetic body.

Seed syllables are ancient sacred formulas known to many cultures. In one respect, they represent the beginnings of language and are unique to the human experience. When we speak or chant these potent combinations of consonants and vowels, we open ourselves to awakening a quality or power and, in many traditions, the divine energy of a deity that already lives within. The mind focuses on the sound production of a particular syllable in order to evoke and embody a particular deity, such as Saraswati, the Hindu goddess of music and the arts. One of the seed syllables that invokes her qualities is *aim* (*"ah-eem"*).

Tenzin Wangyal Rinpoche, lineage holder of the ancient Tibetan Bön tradition, speaks of a commentary in one of their most profound texts, the Mother Tantra, which describes the genesis of seed syllables in this way: "From the body of the unborn essence arises the sphere of light, and from that sphere of light arises wisdom. From the wisdom arises the seed syllable and from the seed syllable arises the complete mandala, the deity and the retinue."[3]

Rinpoche goes further to describe the phenomenon of seed syllables in terms readily understood by the contemporary

Western mind. Just as radios and television sets tune into particular frequencies that already exist in space, we are able to tune into the particular exalted qualities embodied in the sound. We don't have to invent or create these frequencies or qualities; they already exist within us. With practice, we can upgrade our receiver from a fuzzy old black-and-white TV to a modern high-definition home-theatre system with surround sound. In any case, the frequencies remain the same, but our experience of them can be greatly enhanced.

The Five Seed Syllables of the Warrior Mind come from the Bön tradition. It is one of the oldest practices where sound meets duration to become a medium for liberating the mind. It is an essential practice that we do over and over in the Yoga of the Voice program. During this practice, we clear the mind, open the throat, warm the heart, ripen the qualities of clarity, love, and openness in our belly, and plant the seed for spontaneous manifestation of rightful action. You can find out more about this powerful practice in *Tibetan Sound Healing* by Tenzin Wangyal Rinpoche.[4]

As we discussed in the previous chapter, we call these syllables "seeds," or bija in Sanskrit, because when we intone them, they emulate the moment of conception of female and male energy in the production of sound: the vowels are the open, receptive, female aspect; the consonant is the more piercing, powerful male aspect of the sound. By sounding the syllable we bring our awareness into felt experience, supporting our internal process of opening the voice with our sustained concentration on the syllable.

Dhrupad is a vocal genre in Hindustani classical music, said to be the oldest and most erudite still in use in that musical tradition. If I were allowed to sing only one form of music for the rest of my life, I would be divinely happy singing just dhrupad. The sound of dhrupad singing is mostly achieved by singing seed syllables. Dhrupad singers start with a primordial mantra, such as "Ananda Hari Om," and deconstruct it, dissecting it into separate sounds for each syllable of the sacred word, with undulating variations of tone until it is no longer recognizable, yet deeply felt. You can refer to this practice in chapter 6, page 96.

Chanting seed syllables is the best possible preliminary practice to activate the voice. These condensed sounds are charged with secret frequencies; singing them with short tones suggests movement and action. Intoning them long and slowly allows us to enter fully in the realm of selflessness: *who is singing?*

On a metaphysical level, the conscious energy in a seed sound rapidly moves prana through the body, resulting in a sense of increased balance, concentration, union, and relaxation—the formula for well-being. The qualities evoked tend to be protecting, revitalizing, and awakening. You are on the fast track—everything happens in an instant.

Rinpoche offers us this explanation:

> The Mother Tantra describes specific sound practices to treat physical ailments such as headaches, chest pain, and other problems. The right sounds create balance between the five elements of earth, water, fire, air, and space. These elements, present in nature, are also present in each one of us . . . so maintaining this balance is essential to good health. There are practices of chanting certain sounds, certain syllables, which activate or pacify each of the elements. These have a subtle but potent effect on our organs, and on our mental and spiritual states . . . These seed sounds contain elemental qualities that vibrate different parts of the body and different chakras . . . As our chakras are affected in this way, a higher vibration may be activated.[5]

Seed syllables also provide an opportunity for extending the repertory of practices we share with others. This book offers practices from various cultures that implement seed syllables and seed sounds as vibrational formulas: Hindu (see Brahm, the Creator in chapter 6, page 97, and Bija Syllables in chapter 6, page 98), African and Afro-Brazilian (see Inward Singing in chapter 5, page 69), and the Tibetan practice that follows in this chapter.

You don't need to be a musician to sing seed syllables. In the beginning, it's good to become familiar with seed sounds from traditional practices. They come to us already charged with the healing power of lineage, and they become a rapid vehicle to activate the same strength in ourselves. After a few months of doing these traditional practices, you may be inspired to research potent seed sounds from your own cultural back-ground, and don't be surprised if you find yourself resonating with spontaneously occurring seed sounds that spring from awakened consciousness. You may notice that these sounds empower your body and mind when you feel weak or vulner-able; if so, make them part of your private dialect. Spirituality can be personal and "vocal."

▶ Listen to track 16: Elemental Seed Sounds

exercise 33 **Elemental Seed Sounds**

These single-syllable sounds connect with and transform energy. The following practices—from Tibetan (demonstrated on the accompanying audio) and Hindu sources—are as enduring and evolving as the traditions they come from. Other sources might indicate different correlations between the syllables and specific organs, chakras, or qualities. Feel free to choose the associa-tions that resonate the most with you.

1. Start by selecting any of the following seed syllables and bring your attention to the quality of tone you wish to bring forth and the area of the body you want to influence.

2. As you slowly chant the seed sound, connect your breath with sound and sound with your body. Allow for deep resonance with the effortless tone of your voice, chanting the syllable melodiously, again and again. Let it be long.

From the Tibetan tradition—Seed sounds that purify the elements:

E (pronounced "eh")
  Space

Yam (pronounced "yahm" with emphasis on the "ah")
  Air—Lungs

Bam (pronounced "bahm" with emphasis on the "ah")
  Water—Blood

Ram (pronounced "rahm" with emphasis on the "ah")
  Fire—Stomach

Lam (pronounced "lahm" with emphasis on the "ah")
  Earth—Root, spine

From the Hindu tradition—Seed sounds that connect the physical with the subtle body and balance the chakras:

Lam (pronounced "lahm" with emphasis on the "ah")
  Root chakra—promotes security

Vam (pronounced "vahm" with emphasis on the "ah")
  Sacral chakra—promotes fluidity and creativity

Ram (pronounced "rahm" with emphasis on the "ah")
  Navel chakra—builds grounding, confidence

Yam (pronounced "yahm" with emphasis on the "ah")
Heart chakra—balances emotions

Ham (pronounced "hahm" with emphasis on the "ah")
Throat—frees self-expression

Om
Third eye—restores balance and serenity

Ah
Crown chakra—connects with the eternal

INVOCATION

Invocation invites us to enter devotionally into the space of music. While working with seed syllables allows us to connect with energies, deities, and the elements, an invocation is a direct call for a beneficial quality to be manifested through sound.

Drawing on words of power, seed syllables, deity calls, magic sounds, and divine utterances, all spiritual traditions of enlightenment have used invocation as a primordial gateway to transcendence. Through invocation, we call in spirit and the divine attributes to be manifested, recognizing that these are aspects of our higher selves in harmonious synergy with the entire web of life.

Invocations are essential for experiencing the expressiveness of the human voice, transforming exhalation into a longing for the deeper spiritual aspirations. In invocation, we hear a variety of utterances that may sound like praise, a joyful call, a cry for peace, clamors, or a yearning for deliverance through sound and sorrow.

When we chant seed syllables, our focus is inward, often on a particular location in the physical body (organs) or ethereal body (chakras). Invocation, on the other hand, propels the voice outward, creating a bridge between inner and outer worlds of sound.

We are inviting a deity to come and sit next to us. Already energetically engaged, we are ready to bring the quality we aim for into our mind and body. We are actually invoking the name of a deity, not just a sound—and some kind of transformation is the result. We allow ourselves to become someone else. Musically, we can think of an invocation as having the force and direction of an arrow, reaching straight out for a particular power or quality to be embodied through sound.

As a vocalist, composer, and voice educator, I know of no musical tradition that does not include invocation as an integral part of its repertoire of vocal arts. Invocation is also the preliminary stage of every chanted spiritual practice.

In my music, invocation is the natural doorway to the mystery of inspiration; it readies my sensibility to the appropriate devotional feeling, such as affection, compassion, and gratitude. Invocation permeates consciousness with confidence and the release of boundless radiance, openness, and love. Its subtle and slow variations help tune our auditory perception to fine microtones, making the experience of chanting intensely spiritual and revealing.

From the core of the Self, invocation emerges as the exalted cry for connection with the essence of all things, preparing us to receive knowledge of the true nature of inner relationships.

exercise 34 Invocation Practices

The following invocations are from three different traditions of sacred sound. Listen to the audio tracks, which demonstrate the pronunciation and melody for each of the three invocations. Play the audios again and again, singing along with them until you memorize them and make them your own. Then feel free to improvise the melodies and create your own invocations.

Tibetan Invocation to Green Tara

Om Tare Tutare Ture Swaha

▶ Listen to track 17: Tibetan Invocation to Green Tara

Invocation to Oxalá, the divinity of light and father of human-kind in the Yoruba tradition

▶ Listen to Track 18: Yoruba Invocation to Orishá Oxalá

This is a traditional chant for Oxalá, sung by Edvaldo Araujo Alabe.

Hindu Invocation to the Divine Mother

▶ Listen to track 19: Hindu Invocation to the Divine Mother

> *Ananda Mai*
> *Chaitanya Mai*
> *Satya Mai*
> *Paramai*

"O Thou full of bliss, full of consciousness, full of truth, supreme." Translated by Sri Aurobindo.

VOCAL MEDITATION

Having reached out and opened to receiving all the enlighten-ing sounds with invocation, we arrive at the heart of the Yoga of the Voice, its signature piece, which we call vocal meditation. Vocal meditation *is* the journey we've been preparing for. This is the most desired singing experience of voice yogis.

With vocal meditation, we embark on a musical field trip where the most important concern is how we move leisurely from one note to another and how we approach each individual note. This is an upgrade to our software—enabling us to go beyond the adventure of tone to a conscious investigation and sculpting of notes. Unlike tone, which we discussed as a sound conveying meaning and consciousness, a musical note has no intrinsic meaning. It only has meaning in relationship with other notes. Music is the art of arranging notes—up and down and around. The art of singing is about carefully approaching one note and then the next, searching for form, truth, and beauty.

Toning and vocal meditation complement each other. Whereas toning is relaxing and clearing, vocal meditation completes the journey by fine-tuning and developing a path for the voice.

The practice of vocal meditation consists in singing with a drone—a continuous sound that contains myriad harmonics and overtones. The drone becomes our home in this practice, and our intention is to dwell there for a long time until we are ready to slowly venture forth. When we are ready, the voice moves at a very slow pace from one note to another note, exploring the directions of up and down. It is like tuning an instrument, unhurriedly feeling your way up and down the scale.

We explore the art of *meending,* traveling to the spaces in between the notes. In North Indian music, meend is the art of connecting notes. We can visualize our voice as a cello string and approach each note as a complete piece of music in itself, sliding into and out of it. Western music refers to this as *portamento.* We also call it microtonal singing.

Mathieu describes this beautifully: "Meend vivifies melodies, making them sanguine and glossy and velvety by turns, saturating them with feeling. Even a small dose of this practice can significantly change the way you listen to music, especially sung music, by opening up the deep world that lies underneath the surface."[6]

In the Hindustani tradition of classical music, a similar practice of vocal meditation is called *alap.* In this tradition, the exploration serves as an invitation to a raga—a particular tonal arrangement of notes from the Indian tradition, which we will talk about later in the next chapter. We don't need to know the ragas to practice vocal meditation, but a raga may come to visit *us,* if we are familiar with its specific melody. It's not the destination of the journey, but we may just end up there.

In vocal meditation, we start a musical journey, but we don't yet know the destination. We begin innocently—wandering through a tonal landscape we've never been to before, moving slowly until some melody soars through the mind like a bird. It keeps coming back. So we pay attention, carefully, like an architect deciding where to place a building's front entrance. Then we may discover that this melody brings with it a specific scale (or a mode) to build on. So we decide to commit to the musical path that has opened. It feels natural and inspiring to the voice.

In our gentle dance with sound, vocal meditation prepares our musical imagination to receive and remember divinely inspired melodies. We simply witness as melodic movements unfold naturally; we listen carefully and explore movement like a choreographer creating a dance or a bird making a nest. At some point in the journey, we fall in love and allow ourselves to be carried by the emotional beauty of just one melody. This melody makes a big impact, and we are not the same. Now we have a map and we want to visit all possible combinations of this one melody.

In vocal meditation, we want the voice to be liquid. How does water move? Fluidly. It flows freely and doesn't want to stop. It can move very slowly, softly, so minimally it can only be detected by the shifting light. The movement of the voice belongs essentially to the element of water. In this, we may invoke again Saraswati—the Hindu goddess of knowledge, music, and the arts—whose name means "she who flows and endows beauty and wisdom to all things that sound." Saraswati is the reigning deity, the patron goddess, of the Yoga of the Voice.

The slow *glissando*—the buttery, wavering motion of the voice as it approaches one note from another—conveys deep emotion, giving rise to feelings often unassociated with any-thing in particular. Through vocal meditation, we welcome our emotional landscape, tune the voice with the body, and create a path from tone to melody.

This is improvisation. It is open space. Enjoy the ride—but please listen when the teacher within says to go slowly and take pleasure in the silence in between. Something like this: sing, don't sing, listen, listen to the silence. Then . . . sing, don't sing, listen. Silence is your best friend.

▶ Listen to track 20: Vocal Meditation Practice

exercise 35 Vocal Meditation Practice

This practice requires a drone. You can use a sruti box, harmo-nium, tamboura, raagini box, or track 2 of the audio download.

1. Start by humming. Visualize a calm river moving infinitely slow.

2. Slowly open your lips, dwelling in one note and then another note. Use simple syllables to begin with, such as *ah, naa, ree,* and *tom.*

3. Let each note become a chant, a comfortable abode, as you make minimal steps up and down the scale.

4. Go back to something you like—repeating until you find one particular melody to adore and adorn.

5. Journey.

6. At the end of the journey, come back to the root tone. Doesn't it feel good to come home?

Mantra

At some point in our gentle meandering through vocal meditation, we may notice ourselves finding a melody that grooves in
a loop we really like. The groove is in the mind, guiding us right
into the territory of mantra.

If singing is food for the brain, mantras are the power bars.
If you sing a sacred mantra for a long time, you might not need
to do anything else to boost your energy or to relax your mind,
or best of all, to open your heart.

Practitioners of Ayurvedic medicine, an ancient comprehensive
system of medicine from India, often prescribe adaptogens, plants
or herbs that normalize and regulate the systems of the body. This
is how I think about mantras. They can either wake you up or
settle you into sleep, whatever you need. They give you vitality,
they calm you down, and they give you love. "Love is all you
need": that's a beautiful mantra. Perhaps part of The Beatles' suc-
cess is that we can find a hidden mantra in almost all of their songs.

All cultures have mantras, and mantras have many meanings,
or no meaning at all. Basically, a mantra can be any empowered
word or phrase that is chanted repetitively in order to clear
the mind and attain oneness with cosmic consciousness where
infinite bliss abides. In the ancient Eastern tradition (including
India and Tibet), the words or sounds of a mantra are sacred
syllables that contain in their essence divine (or magic) powers.
The repetition of the mantra (*japa*) leads the mind toward the
realization of the principle being evoked by the words, height-
ening consciousness to the appreciation of the sacred.

Many seed syllables can be chanted as a mantra. The most
well-known is *Om*, which represents the entire vibratory
nature of the universe, as we talked about in the previous chapter. Ancient Vedic teachings say that the Om mantra is God in
the form of sound.

Mantras serve as auditory centering devices that have the
power to protect, purify, and transform the emotional state and

consciousness of the individual who repeats them. At the same time, the mental concentration involved in a mantra reawakens energies that recharge the physical body (specifically the brain) and the subtle body (the chakras). Ultimately, mantra chanting induces devotion in the mind of the singer, activating a state of blissful liberation through sound.

If needed, mantras activate healing, as they have the alchemical capacity to transform energy. The sounds themselves are intoned, with the power to purify and protect the one who repeats them—and anyone who is listening. The word *mantra* comes from two Sanskrit roots meaning "protection" and "mind." So, quite literally, mantras are "protectors for the mind." In his illuminating book *Mantra and Meditation,* Pandit Usharbudh Arya describes how a mantra that is kept in the mind serves as protection from the six internal mental enemies: passions, anger, greed, attachment, jealousy, pride (or malice). By repetition and concentration, the mantra serves as an antidote to these enemies.[7]

The more we connect subtly with the movement of the mantra, the more we can feel it spin like a wheel. In my experience, mantras are like sonic chakras, or wheels of power. The beauty of chanting a mantra is that we don't really need to know what it means to get the effect. The transformative power of the mantra lies in the sound of the words and the fully conscious mind of the user. I like to think of mantra as abstract art, leaving it open to interpretation. This allows the mind to groove freely, detached from meaning and culture. When we release the need to know what the words mean, we are truly in the affective dimension of mantra. Our mind has been purified. The mirror is clean.

This explains why, in the Buddhist tradition, mantra chanting is used as a device to overcome attachments and conditioning throughout our journey of spiritual liberation. By the combination of breath and sound, mantra chanting clears the movements of the mind, allowing the mind to reveal its true nature: emptiness and clarity.

exercise 36 Mantra Practices

The following mantras may be spoken or sung. An audio track is provided for each one. Play each track again and again, and sing along with it until you memorize it and make it your own. Then feel free to improvise and create your own melodies or mantras.

Tibetan mantra for the embodiment of compassion:

Om Mani Padme Hum

▶ Listen to track 21: Tibetan Mantra: *Om Mani Padme Hum*

Hindu mantra calling the divine name of Amma, the avatar of the goddess Narayani

Om Sree Amma Narayani Namastute

▶ Listen to track 22: Hindu Mantra: *Om Sree Amma Narayani Namastute*

Tibetan Invocation to Green Tara

Om Tare Tutare Ture Swaha

▶ Listen to track 17: Tibetan Invocation to Green Tara

PRAYER

> *To open the gates of trust in God, nothing can*
> *replace the beauty of human voices united in song.*
> THE TAIZE BROTHERHOOD

Another potential for musical exploration with the voice is prayer. Prayer is unique in that it conveys a request, a thanksgiving, or an honoring to whatever higher power we believe in. A mantra can be a prayer, but unlike mantra, the affective power of prayer does not require repetition, just a petition.

I very much like the description of prayer from Sister Joan Chittister, a Benedictine nun and international advocate for peace:

> My definition of prayer is consciousness, immersion, and relationship. Prayer makes us aware of the elements of the divine in human life, bringing us into contact with the God-life in and around us. Prayer is not personal devotion; it is personal growth. Prayer brings us to the ultimate and the eternal, the daily and the regular, the total consciousness of God now. Prayer enables us to be immersed in what is fundamentally and truly divine in life right now.[8]

Singing a prayer brings us closer to what we believe (or what we believe that we believe). *Belief is energy* and, as such, can be a powerful instrument for transformation and inner serenity. If we come from a tradition of sung or even spoken prayer, bringing those remembered words and memories into our practice forges a link with our ancestral lineage.

Many cultures have songs that, when needed, become prayers. Like mantras, these song prayers have the power to move us devotionally, even if we don't know the language or traditions that inspired them. The Yoga of the Voice welcomes a trans-cultural repertoire of prayers that are constructed with a simple melody, sung softly, and accompanied with words or poetry in various languages that clearly express an intention. For some, singing *is* prayer—as in the music of the Taizé community (an ecumenical community in Burgundy, France) with its repetitive phrases, where the voice can be a cappella or have a background of drones or a minimal harmonic progression.

A common practice of our students is self-generated prayer, an improvisational prayer that emerges spontaneously as an expression of longing. The inspired words of prayers, combined with background music and textures of the voice, take us to a greater dimension.

exercise 37   Self-Generated Prayer

The essence of self-generated prayer is stream of consciousness, stepping out of the way, and letting your words pour out spontaneously.

1. Sit quietly, inviting a quality of reverence and devotion to arise.

2. Bring to mind something that you are grateful for. Let the quality of gratitude expand and open your heart.

3. When you are ready, allow words to come. Consider starting with a simple "thank you," in any language, repeating as often as you like.

4. As you get in the groove, allow your spontaneous gratitude to flow in words. Add melody and rhythm if you like.

5. Afterward, sit in silence with the confidence that your prayer has been heard.

▶ Listen to track 23: Vedic Prayer for Peace and Well-Being

exercise 38 Vedic Prayer for Peace
and Well-Being

This daily prayer reminds us that our relationships with all beings and things should be mutually beneficial if we ourselves desire happiness and liberation from suffering. This Hindu prayer is usually recited after most rituals and meditations. The audio will guide you in the pronunciation of the words.

Lokah Samasta Sukinho Bhavantu
Om Shanti, Shanti, Shanti

"May all beings everywhere be happy and free, and may the thoughts, words, and actions of my own life contribute in some way to that happiness and to that freedom for all. Peace, Peace, Peace."

CHANT

Chanting is a significant and mysterious practice. It is the highest nectar, a tonic that fully nourishes our inner being. Chanting opens the heart and makes love flow within us.
SWAMI MUKTANANDA

So far, our tour of the Yoga of the Voice operating system has introduced us to breath, sound, tone, seed syllables, invocation, vocal meditation, mantra, and prayer. Chanting is all of these:

deep and shared breath

inspired sound

a firing of seed syllables that burns into sacredness

the invocation of divine qualities we desire to manifest

a journey of vocal meditation that finds the sweetest melody

the repetition of a mantra that turns into a request

a selfless state of prayer that evolves in form and color

Chanting encompasses the vast territory of the vocal arts. It is born at that precise moment when we encounter a contagious melody—familiar or new—that calls us to explore limitless possibilities of melodic variation. The resulting practice might sound like a ballad, a song, a hymn, an aria, a raga, or a tune. All is chanting when the clear heart of improvisation takes over our imagination.

This is the essence of chanting: a spirited short song with a fixed melody that transcends time, yet is open to melodic variations and harmonies. With its simple form and endless variety, the chant itself inspires us to share it with others. We want to offer it, to give it away to all.

Although a seed syllable or a mantra may also be chanted, what we refer to as a chant has a beginning and an end, more variations, more room for improvisation, and possibly a fixed form. A chant may use words, tell a story, or sound like a song. It may even have a composer. It may involve a request or express gratitude, often shared communally. A chant is usually short and memorable—as intoxicating as perfume.

Just in case you were wondering about the difference between singing and chanting, there is none. I firmly believe that if you can talk, you can chant—and when you chant, you are singing. Chanting and singing are as old as humankind. With such ancient forms, all differences fade.

Don Campbell, author of *The Mozart Effect,* affirms that "Chant is not an obscure musical ritual—it is an important tool used by people everywhere to heal their bodies, quiet their minds, and bring the sacred into their lives. . . . It brings people together in thought, intention, and love."[9] Lately, world news reveals chanting to be a unifying tool for collective peacemaking or a nonviolent way to depose a dictator.

As a devotional practice, chanting has been preserved for centuries and can be found in all cultures. The rhythm of devotional chant is repetitive, with subtle alterations of tempo, pace, and pulse. The sacred meaning of the words or syllables adds to the magnetic and ecstatic effect enhanced by the group sound. God is everywhere, as George Harrison lovingly reminds us in his soulful modern chant, "My Sweet Lord."[10]

As a musician and sound artist, my dearest and most sophisticated practice is raga chanting. Singing ragas, whether solo or in a group, is both exquisitely challenging and gratifying. Every time I sing a raga, I sing it differently, although it might be the same raga or melodic arrangement. Chanting ragas is so humbling, so unpredictable, because the intervals between the notes arise from pure inspiration. And regardless of age or history, ragas always feel like new compositions—a perfect balance between improvisation and form, mantra, invocation, chant, and vocal meditation.

Chanting the ragas, when all is perfectly in tune, makes me feel like I live in a world of boundless beauty. This is what I have in common with George Harrison and jazz saxophonist John Coltrane: we fell in love with the ragas.

Chanting is an extremely satisfying sensory experience that can purify our senses and emotions, as well as our surroundings, and lead us naturally to contentment or contemplation. The healing power of the voice finds its fullest expression through chanting.

Ultimately, the Yoga of the Voice integrates all vocal arts, aiming to vitalize all kinds of chanting, where the divide between the sacred and the profane is lifted. We welcome any musical material that offers a glimpse of the divine, goose bumps of ecstasy, and a liberating state of spiritual joy.

Chanting in groups—blending one's own voice with other voices—creates a sense of supreme well-being. However, the

most advanced practice I can recommend is private chanting—
that sublime moment when, in the absolute intimacy of your
practice room, you pick up a drone instrument, tune it, breathe
deeply, and dwell in one note, smooth and long. This is your time
to bask in musical vibrations, revitalizing the body-mind—for a
minimum of twenty-one minutes—in the all-embracing experience from breath to chant. Allow yourself the luxury of getting
knowingly lost, and dwell in the deep silence that follows.

exercise 39 Chant Practices

Here are two chants, one from the Peruvian Amazon and one
from the Hindu tradition.

Icaro del Silbido

▶ Listen to track 24: Icaro del Silbido: Peruvian Amazon
Healing Song

Peruvian Amazon *icaros* are medicine melodies with profound
consciousness-altering effects. These are songs the plants themselves "transmit" to Amazonian healers once they are physically,
mentally, and spiritually prepared to receive them. The accompanying audio features a chant comprised of vocal sounds and
whistles.

Chant of Dedication: Twameva Mata

▶ Listen to track 25: Chant of Dedication: Twameva Mata

This traditional Hindu dedication is usually recited at the con-
clusion of a prayer session, meditation, or religious function.
Here the devotee surrenders his or her individuality to the Lord
for his Grace.

Twameva Mata Chapita Twameva
Twameva Bandhu Cha Sakha Twameva
Twameva Vidya Dravinam Twameva
Twameva Sarvam Mama Deva Deva

"O God,
You are my mother, my father, my brother, and my friend.
You are my knowledge and my only wealth.
You are everything to me and the God of all Gods."

――――――――

8

Music à la Mode

*The work of the musician consists . . . only
in knowing, as accurately as possible, the
symbolic relation of all things so as to
reproduce in us, through the magic of sounds,
the feelings, the passions, the visions of an
almost real world.*
ALAIN DANIÉLOU, *Sacred Music*

The possibilities of the voice are open to anybody—of
any age, any background, and any musical experience. Everyone at every level has the tools to grow in awareness, connection, and expression through the Yoga of the Voice practice.
On this path, a deeply felt and long *ah* may center your being
and set the perfect mood, in a few seconds.

Sooner or later, as part of the creative process, we may
want to enrich our practice by inviting more elements of
music and music-making into our experience. By familiar-
izing ourselves with the architecture of music and the basic
components of music theory, we expand our skill and open

to greater potential. Adding these elements is like putting ice cream on the cake.

The more we know about music, the easier it becomes to share with others, and vice versa. By exchanging our musical energy with others—whether a single individual or a group of any size—we have more opportunities for creative expression. As my colleague Rick Jarow, who teaches people how to reach their highest potential, says, "Creativity is not an individual process."

The collective process of creativity, as I see it, involves other people as well as all the resources we can collectively gather. In this chapter I offer you the dessert tray: tasty bits of musical information to get your creativity flowing. I also invite you to gather information from books by legendary masters of music, from the Internet, and through *lots* of repetition.

Collaboration, repetition, knowledge, devotional dedication, musical languages from other cultures can take your singing as far as your dreams—nourishing your aspirations and charming the world around you. Don't give up! Sometimes enlightenment requires a little bit of effort.

Sargam: A Musical Alphabet

I experience music as the language of the heart, a true universal language that helps us communicate when words are insufficient to express what we want to say or sing. Every language, including the language of music, starts with an alphabet.

The alphabet we use as part of the Yoga of the Voice comes from Hindustani or North Indian classical music. It is referred to as the *sargam* or *saregama*. The sargam is simply the practice of singing the names of the notes in Sanskrit, as a reliable stairway to go up and down the scales. Our nearest equivalent in the West is the *solfeggio* (do re mi fa sol la ti), a technique for the teaching of sight singing. The sargam, however, has more ancient and cosmic roots. It comes from the Samaswara system, which dates from the late Vedic period (around 1000

BC), whereas the European solfeggio was invented in the tenth century AD. For many students, teachers, and experienced musicians as well, the singing of the notes through the sargam is the most captivating part of the practice.

The sargam syllables were and are used for tuning and opening the voice, which is considered the most essential performer of Indian classical music, while the solfeggio was originally developed for sight singing, dictation, and learning songs typically accompanied by instruments. The syllables of the sargam are abbreviated from Sanskrit names for the seven principal notes (or *swaras*) of the scale and are sung as *Sa, Re, Ga, Ma, Pa, Dha, Ni* and written in musical notation as S, R, G, M, P, D, N. The word sargam is an acronym of the first four syllables. The sargam is a system of notation; it is also a composition in which the words are the names of the notes.

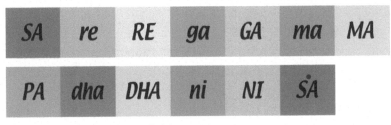

Figure 1: The sargam syllables

With the sargam, the emphasis is on the intervals and the space in between each note in relation to the other. The tone *Sa* is movable—it is not assigned to a specific pitch, and it can be any note of the scale. Sa is our foundation, the root, or the tonic of a scale. All the other swaras are sung in relationship to Sa, making it a fixed tonic, or tonal center. In Sanskrit, Sa comes from the word *sadja*—*sad* means "six" and *aja* means "creator of"—Sa literally gives birth to the other six swaras.

My teacher, maestro Ali Akbar (also affectionately called Khansahib), frequently used the metaphor of Sa as the mother—the home from which we depart and to which we always return—and Pa as the father—the one who keeps the equilibrium throughout the path of the scale. Together they represent the perfect union of the Hindu deities Shiva and Shakti, the divine couple, where Shiva corresponds to the masculine principle and Shakti the feminine principle. Musically, Sa and Pa create the interval of the perfect fifth. This means they are always natural (*shuddha,* or "pure"), never sharp or flat. As Khansahib would say, "Like your mother and your father, Sa and Pa never change." We can count on Sa and Pa to be our guiding lights when we sing. The other five notes can be altered: re, ga, dha, and ni can be natural or flat (*komal*), and ma can be natural or sharp (*tivra*). Ma is the only note in the scale that can be sharp. The addition of flat and sharp notes gives us the twelve notes that are relatively equal to our Western chromatic scale.

In the notation we use, capital letters are used for Sa and Pa and for the pure/natural form of the note. Lower-case letters indicate the lower form. Hence, S R G m P D N represents the major scale we are accustomed to in the West. In the major scale, all the notes are natural or shuddha; ma is written in lower case because the natural ma—the exception—is closer to Sa than its alternate, tivra (sharp) Ma.

The entire sargam can be written as follows: S r R g G m M P d D n N Ṡ representing the twelve notes of the chromatic scale. (The dot on the top of the final S indicates that it is an octave higher than the original S; a lower octave would be indicated by a dot underneath the note. The dots are used above or below the letter to indicate a higher or lower octave respectively.)

Indian music is such a good mother that she has more to give than just twelve notes. In addition to the twelve notes available in the Western chromatic scale, Hindustani music invites us to explore twenty-two microtones. These are called srutis, precise microtonal variations that exist between the notes. Thus, the sargam teaches us to pay attention to the "space between," where transformation and healing can take place. The word *sruti* means "that which is heard" or "that which can be revealed." The musical implication is that the srutis—the space between the notes—carry the wisdom of all that has been revealed through music to humans. The experience of the srutis is the link that connects the voice with consciousness and other extra-musical realms. The srutis and the practice of deep listening live in the same house.

Why are we in love with the sargam? Because it transmits so much—so much insight, so much possibility, so much connection to the natural world. Every time we practice the sargam, we experience the return to childlike innocence. It always feels new and inspires fresh listening while precisely aligning and boosting our musical memory (the ability to remember music-related information, such as melodic content and other progressions of tones or pitches).

The sargam unveils and embodies the cosmic nature of music. The word *swara* (which refers to the principal notes of the sargam) comes from the Sanskrit roots *swa* (self) and *ra* (illumination). Swara, therefore, is an utterance expressing the potential for personal enlightenment, and the sargam constitutes the link between the musical notes and the Self.

The sargam also reveals the intimate connection between music and nature. Besides corresponding to notes, each shuddha swara originates from the sound of a different bird or animal. Sa comes from the sound of the peacock, re from the skylark, ga from the goat, ma from the dove or heron, Pa from the nightingale, dha from the horse, and ni from the elephant. The sargam also corresponds to colors of light and particular constellations of stars. It is like singing the alphabet of the spirit world, and it can be experienced in gross, subtle, and extra-subtle levels of consciousness—an animated way for the voice to connect with the highest textures of reality.

Singing the notes of the sargam can profoundly affect the subtle energy centers of the body. Many singers and teachers choose to enforce the correspondence and associate a particular note with a particular chakra. This may seem attractive, but it comes from a superficial understanding. Through my across-the-borders experience, I realize that any note has the potential to connect with any center of subtle energy according to the particular mood, body, and circumstance of each individual. Why limit the affective capacity of these generous musical entities?

Mostly we love to sing the sargam syllables for the relationship we cultivate with pure *sound*. With its inspiration directly from the natural world, the sargam allows for freer, more intuitive movement of the voice. The vowels are open, wide, and quite effective for tuning the voice with the ear—and the ear with the voice. Because we don't have preconceptions concerning these sounds in the West, intoning them tends to free us from impediments or any mental concerns. They offer the most effective ear training I have ever experienced. The slow singing and modulating of these swaras and srutis feels like devotional chanting—it is simple, controlled, and balanced—always leaving us wanting more. Chanting in sargam is both a necessary and an intellectually fulfilling practice.

We sing the sargam syllables slowly in connection with a particular scale, accompanied by a background drone that plays a combination of the Sa and Pa ratio. Besides facilitating articulation and lessening vocal effort, singing these syllables improves our capacity for auditory perception and aural differentiation. It makes us eager to develop a musical grammar that combines intervals, melodies, and rhythmic formulas.

Each syllable of the sargam is a seed that carries the potential to convey sacred information. As we repeat this practice over and over, we start listening to and attracting the subtle, magical vibrations of the srutis (microtones), the notes in between the notes, the sound that can be revealed, an experience of tone that brings insight into the realm of sacred sound. Therefore, in the Yoga of the Voice the singing of the sargam is the piece that never fails to transmit the experience of the three sounds: the outer, the inner, and the secret sound. When we sing sargam, the body responds to an ancient call from nature, the mind feels lighter, and we attune to a musical language so profound it cannot be conveyed in writing.

MELODY: HORIZONTAL MUSIC

Knowing that music is a language, we shall seek at first to make melody "speak." The melody is the point of departure. May it remain sovereign! . . . The noblest element of music.
OLIVIER MESSIAEN, *The Technique of My Musical Language*

What is it that makes music such an inspiring presence in our lives? Music enthusiasts—even the sublime maestros—agree that music is the most emotionally direct art we have. Since our beginnings, music has always been a means for expressing meaning and feeling, and the melody is simply the most affective and effective attribute of music that touches us and can transform our being immediately.

Melody lays the groundwork for the journey that will transport us to other worlds. It carries the emotional substance, stirs memories, tells a story, and conveys meaning, especially when the melody is rendered by the expressive power of the voice.

In my experience of the singing voice, melody is like a magnet that attracts spiritual energy. It's contagious. We move from one state to another as a familiar melody tells us something about ourselves we long to remember. Melody is the aspect of music that evokes memories associated with powerful life experiences. There's a cultural aspect to this as well. Recently, I was watching a TV special starring Barbra Streisand singing her top ten tunes from the 1970s for an intimate celebrity audience. In minutes, we (myself and the TV personalities) all had tears in our eyes remembering those moments so dear to us. Even after a hard day's work, we can instantly shift our emotional disposition as music brings us back to a personal story that we feel anew.

Memorable melodies can make our lives more meaningful and, ultimately, healthier. On the physical level, melody lights up our brain. Listening to a significant melody vividly activates the brain's many different processing centers, from the auditory cortex to the various centers that deal with emotion and pleasure. The frontal cortex, the same part of the brain that stores working memories and plans complex cognitive behaviors, also plays a big role in melody perception. It makes sense that melody-centered therapies (discussed in chapter 2) are used so successfully with patients suffering from brain damage (such as stroke survivors and Alzheimer's patients, among others).

Melody keeps the brain working in other ways as well, such as playing with our expectations and exciting anticipation, according to Daniel Levitin in his book *This is Your Brain on Music*. He writes:

> Melody is one of the primary ways that our expectations are controlled by composers. Music theorists have identified a principle called gap fill. . . . If the melody makes a big leap, theorists describe a tendency for the melody to "want" to return to the jumping-off point; this is another way to say that our brains expect that the leap was only temporary, and tones that follow need to bring us closer and closer to our starting point, or harmonic 'home.'[1]

Levitin goes on to give examples of how composers from Beethoven to Sting keep us on the edge of our seats by defying our melodic expectations. He continues with the example of the song "Somewhere Over the Rainbow," in which "the melody begins with one of the largest leaps we've ever experienced in a lifetime of music listening: an octave. This is a strong schematic violation, and so the composer rewards and soothes us by bringing the melody back toward home again, but not by too much—he does come down, but only one scale degree—because he wants to build tension. The third note of this melody fills the gap."[2]

So melody can excite and stimulate us, but it also has the power to pacify energy that is agitating the mind. When we are nervous, listening to music can induce a calm feeling. Remember mantras? We sing them over and over, and the senses and the mind get more and more clear of excessive worry. Mantras are so successful in this partly because the melodies are constructed with simplicity and minimalism, involving a great deal of circularity and repetition, with no dramatic leaps. In other words, the brain gets a rest.

In the musical spectrum, melody is defined as a tonal configuration with form and movement that unfolds in relation to time. This is why I like to call it *horizontal music*. Melody unfolds like the waves in the ocean—a horizontal musical line that includes patterns of changing pitch and duration. These are the essential elements of melody, along with timbre, texture, volume, and the feeling that generates mood. All these components create the structural unit we call the *melodic phrase,* a meaningful musical utterance—the storyteller in music and the canvas for the voice.

Here is your new assignment: get a recording device and compile the familiar melodies or songs that are stored in your memory. You can use previously recorded songs, or even better, you can sing them yourself. Treat these melodies with love. This music made you who you are today, and these melodies are part of your biography. Memorable and meaningful melodies will always instigate new music. It's important to have a personal archive to easily access these melodies, with more to come in the future. These melodies are made of "open heart"; sooner or later in your musical life, the melodies will set your voice free.

IN THE MOOD

> *If there is anything at all in this world which
> can change the heart of a man in a very quick
> time, that is music and dance.*
> SWAMI SIVANANDA, *Bliss Divine*

In Indian classical music and early Western music, the treatment of melody was organized around modes. The terms *mode*
and *modal music* are used to define classes of scales and melodies. Modes involve the internal relationship of seven notes at
a time within a scale that might have twelve notes. The pre-
dominant note is the tonic or the key (also tonal center, pedal)
or resting point. The tonic in music is like a tonic you take for
your health: it enlivens and energizes the melodic imagination
by giving the music a sustained ground, a home where notes
can move out, in, around, or even rest, and still belong. The
tonic is the Sa in Indian music.

According to W. A. Mathieu in *The Listening Book,* "Mode
is the direct translation into sound of mood, of indescribable
feeling."[3] Modes and modality are intrinsic to the musical structure of many cultures, such as the Chinese *tyao;* the Arabian
and Turkish *maqam;* the ancient Greek, Gregorian, and medi-
eval chant; Brazilian folk music; Balinese chants; the songs of
the Pygmy people; and the Indian raga mentioned earlier.

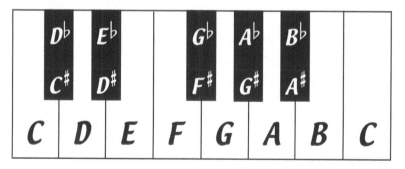

Figure 2: The keyboard of the piano

The classification of the ancient Greek modes differs slightly from the modern system generally taught as part of basic music theory. In the modern approach, the modes are introduced in a key signature that uses all natural notes, with no sharps or flats. The simplest way to understand the relationship of the intervals in each mode is to go to a piano keyboard (you can find one that actually plays on the Internet if you don't have one at home) and listen carefully as you visually connect with the note on the keyboard.

(▶) Listen to track 26: Modes: Using the Keyboard's White Notes

Here's a list of the modes using all the white notes on the keyboard. Play the starting note indicated for each mode (using figure 2 as a guide) and continue playing only the white notes to get the sound of each mode. (You can hear the various modes demonstrated on audio track 26.)

Ionian begins on C. It is identical to our major scale and sounds familiarly sweet and versatile.

Dorian begins on D. The tonality of this minor scale is archetypal; it stirs deep sentiments, with a taste for longing.

Phrygian begins on E. It gives a taste of flamenco . . . and a craving for tapas!

Lydian begins on F. It welcomes the unpredictable.

Mixolydian begins on G. It tastes folksy and makes music that all people love.

Aeolian begins on A. This is our dear natural minor; it's so easy to fall in love with this sound.

Locrian begins on B. It adds a dash of creative dissonance.

Playing only the white notes and proceeding through each degree of the scale is a good way to become familiar with the sonority of the modes. Then you can improvise until your imagination is ready to rest. Another way to play with and understand the modes is by starting any one of them on C and playing the appropriate flats and sharps. Examples follow, but you can research this in greater detail in music theory books or on the Internet. It's important to know that any mode can start on any note. Investigating and memorizing modes (easier than you think!) is a lifelong lesson that keeps you musically sensitive and busy.

▶ Listen to track 27: Modes: Starting on Middle C

Here are the modes starting on middle C. Note that C and G don't have sharps or flats. (These modes are demonstrated on audio track 26.)

Ionian	C D E F G A B C
Dorian	C D E♭ F G A B♭ C
Phrygian	C D♭ E♭ F G A♭ B♭ C
Lydian	C D E F♯ G A B C
Mixolydian	C D E F G A B♭ C
Aeolian	C D E♭ F G A♭ B♭ C
Locrian	C D♭ E♭ F G♭ A♭ B♭ C

According to the ancient Greeks, each mode was considered to have a different impact on the mind of the hearer; Renaissance composers continued this idea. For instance, the Aeolian was considered serious (now we call it "minor" and relate it with qualities of longing) and the Ionian was considered cheerful and suitable only for "frivolous" music. This attitude dated from times when music was solely conceived of as a part of sacred rituals and regal performances. Today, we embrace all the moods and creativity that these modes inspire. We invite all singers of the world to combine them and come up with new, unusual musical moods—as we play music for the awakening of all senses and all sentient beings.

The practice of vocal meditation, accompanied by a sruti box or creating a drone in any instrument, is a good way to get familiar with the distinctive flavor of the different modes. For practitioners who are comfortable using a keyboard, harp, or guitar, I recommend exploring modes in your vocal meditations while you improvise drones on your instrument. I suggest spending time exploring the Dorian, Ionian, Phrygian, and Aeolian modes in particular. These modes have a strong correspondence with ancient Indian ragas implemented for healing.

Don't just play with the modes, leave room for the modes to play with you. If you find yourself falling in love with the Phrygian mode, it may just be that Phrygian (that flirt!) has cast her eye on you. She has been seducing musicians for thousands of years, from Rajasthan to Madrid.

Modal music has the quality of orbital movement, revolving around the tonal center—as if the notes are searching for the still point where everything starts and ends. On the other hand, what we loosely refer to as tonality or tonal music (as opposed to modality and atonal music) gives the impression of a progressive and forward movement that modulates and travels through different tonalities and the tonal centers in a delicate balance between tension and resolution. Tonality, atonality, and modality are systems that probably derived from actual practice—living people making live music. (I say these are loose terms, because modal music also uses tones and tonality but, as Buddha would remind us, "the word is not the thing.")

We emphasize modal music in the preliminary stages of Yoga of the Voice training. Having a tonal center to depart from in addition to a drone in which to dwell helps us engage focus and deep listening. Thus we align and adjust our auditory perception, tune our voice, and comfortably explore the capacity to go up and down as we listen to the same immersive sonic environment. By nature, the singing voice—our invisible musical instrument—unfolds and gets stronger when it goes up and down, up and down, up and down, and all around. This is the core of my spiritual music practice, inspired by an anecdote about Khansahib that has become famous at the Ali Akbar School of Music. When asked whether or not the maestro believed in God, Khansahib paused for some time and finally said softly, "I believe in going up and down the scale."

At the point when practice becomes your sanctuary (and you want to be in that sanctuary often) it is beneficial to challenge yourself by identifying the modes used in familiar songs and to vocalize with these as well. Music composed in different modes can profoundly influence people's emotional and physical states, and it can even shift their state of consciousness. Becoming familiar with the particular modes and their affective quality assists music healers or sound therapists in selecting music appropriate to each situation and mood. Applying these essential aspects of musicianship in your own practice adds enormously to music's therapeutic potential.

In *The Magic of Tone and the Art of Music,* composer and philosopher Dane Rudhyar tells us, "the character of a mode is always, in principle, defined by the nature of the type of emotions it is meant to produce in the hearers. Modes are psychoactive factors." According to Rudhyar, these factors include "the manner in which the successive tones of the melody were approached and the way one tone passed into the next, the vitalization of the tones and the entire melody by the psychic concentration of the singer, the time of day and year, and the environment and circumstances of the performance."[4]

You could spend the rest of your life investigating and singing with these modes as your pathway to making music. You can start creating your own modes, always finding inspiration in the mood that is inside the music. Remember that mood is also a quality of attention. Therefore, the perception and rendering of the right mood for each circumstance will also make you a better person. This is material for many lifetimes. You are drinking from the source of music and healing. You start to wake up to the subtle changes in the quality of light and its relation to changes in emotional disposition. Music makes magic and you are the magician and the healer.

Here's an assignment to make you comfortable with modal magic. Beginning with the second month of each season, select two modes and, starting on different pitches (such as C and E), practice them two times a week. Notice the changes of color and pace in your voice. Dwell in some notes more than others. Sing as you play and play as you sing, always retaining the distinctive modal identity. Afterward, create a mode that represents the mood you would like to be in and see what happens. You are making transformative music. You are in the mood!

THE SEARCH FOR MEANING

Without music life will be a mistake.
FRIEDRICH NIETZSCHE

Modes are made of melodies, and music with a strong melodic component tends to stimulate our longing for vision, meaning, and expression. More and more, I feel an urgency to bring back into the realm of improvisation, composition, and music education the idea that any musical experience can be a journey that actually takes us somewhere—or anywhere where meaning can be enlightening. I am concerned that this aspect is missing in much of the music distributed today through mass media and, while the result can be very pleasing to listen to, we are left without anywhere to go.

Our essential human nature compels us to search for meaning. The conscious treatment of melody encompasses this search, leading the practitioner to ever-higher levels of musical expression. This is the art of melodic narration. In this moving aural architecture, one melody becomes the point of departure and the seed that generates other melodies. A melodic dialogue develops, grows, expands, reaches a peak, returns to the source, and completes itself.

Melodic narration is the poetry within music—when the melody we create is like a poem that builds up and expresses a saga over the airwaves, something deep about the universe and humanity. When notes become words, and words tell the story, moving through layers of harmonies and rhythms, melodies turn into everlasting memories.

This is what the European Romantics and other great masters have taught us. As you listen again to Bach's choral music, Beethoven's string quartets, Mozart's piano concertos, and Mahler's unbearably beautiful symphonies, notice how the music poses the question, "Where are you taking me?" A dialogue has begun. The possibility of orchestral architecture and poetry through sound arises. We are entranced, enthused, and involved. There has to be a moment in music-making when we listen in this way—searching for meaning, transcending personality, and reaching the depth of psychic imagination. Our musicality takes on all the wonder of the universe.

We are now in mythic time. This instant, for me, breaks all conventions: meaning is no meaning. No form becomes form. I am free from melody, harmony, rhythm, and everything. My voice has been liberated from all boundaries, and I am carried away by a wild and enchanting muse. This is music healing at its highest.

HARMONY: VERTICAL MUSIC

Sung harmony is embodied intelligence.

W. A. MATHIEU, *Harmonic Experience*

I hope I have been successful so far in communicating that making music is like being an architect. We are grounding, building, and designing—practicing the art of juxtaposing tones, forms, voices, words, sounds, movement, textures, and vision.

In the realm of making music, it is the horizontal line of melody that expands and creates variations and combinations of notes called countermelodies (secondary melodies sounded afterward or at the same time). These in turn inspire the creation of vertical music: harmony. Harmony is defined as the sounding of notes in a vertical configuration at the same time, with one note being higher or lower than the other. It implies the structural design of chords (notes placed on top of one another) and their movement as chord progressions or broken chords called arpeggios (tones of a chord sounded in succession). While melody moves like the waves of the ocean, harmony aims to connect heaven and earth.

Olivier Messiaen, one of the foremost twentieth-century composers (as well as a celebrated ornithologist and mystic), encourages us not to forget "the natural harmony: the true unique, voluptuously pretty by essence, willed by the melody, issued from it, pre-existing in it, having always been enclosed in it, awaiting manifestation."[5] Messiaen elaborates on his fascination with harmony: "My secret of enchanted gorgeousness in harmony has pushed me toward those swords of fire, those sudden stars, those flows of blue-orange lavas, those planets of turquoise, those violet shades, those garnets of long-haired arborescence, those wheelings of sound and colors in a jumble of rainbows . . ."[6]

In music improvisation and composition (which can be regarded as improvisation in slow motion), melody tells the story while harmony, willed by the melody, amplifies, expands, and colors the musical space, transcending the personal quality of melody and taking us toward the collective. Singing in harmony demands that we carefully listen to other voices. This, in itself, can be so profound. Sometimes, spontaneous harmonies sound like the resonance of invisible choirs, voices like those we hear in dreams.

Historically, the progressive use of harmony reflected the evolution of musical complexity and aesthetics, giving birth to polyphony (two or more independent melodic voices or a multiplicity of instruments). This, in turn, gave rise to infinite musical possibilities, reaching harmonic height in our magnificent symphonic passages, where the shamanic force of music meets the boundless frontiers of human imagination.

Harmony can either sound natural and follow the "rules" (what we call "consonant"), or it can sound dissonant and create tension, expectation, and suspense by transcending rules and stylistic boundaries. Harmony can be light, with just a few notes happening at the same time—like the delicate color-chords inspired by birdsong in Messiaen's astonishing composition, *Oiseaux Exotiques*—or textural, chromatic, and dense, as in the other-worldly dissonant choral music by György Ligeti.

The genius composer Bach in a way melodized harmony and harmonized melodies. In his music, almost every melodic line suggests a harmonic accompaniment and carries the same emotional content. Harmony was in the air for Johann Sebastian; he approached it as science, as religion, and as a healing art in times of great personal despair. His precise balance between melodic themes, narration, and harmonic expansion makes the beauty and timelessness of his music.

In the context of healing through music and singing, the use of harmony benefits from the same mindfulness we apply to the use of melody. It is contingent upon the intention and the circumstance. For example, if we are offering music at the bedside of an ailing person or assisting at the end of life, the music might be slow and meandering; it doesn't need to "go some-where" harmonically. We can offer music that features sparse and ethereal melodies that gradually develop into resonant and subtle harmonic progressions with a transporting, timeless quality in their motion. Such harmonies convey changelessness and the calm passage of time. I refer to this treatment as *tran-scendent harmonies;* as the notes and chords change slowly, the harmonies are revealed through seemingly transparent drones. The voice goes along with the journey, gentle and soft, with a spiritual reverence for space. Like the energy of the healer, the voice is always listening, and *being* more than *doing.*

To get a sense of how to embody transcendent harmonies, you can practice by listening and singing with a drone instru-ment or a sruti box with the tonic and the fourth or fifth note open. (Or you can use tuning forks if you have them— preferably two different forks such as C and G to create the interval of the fifth.) Simply listen closely to the subtle differ-ence between the two notes, and rest in the sound inside the interval. Then sing something with it that sounds and feels good. Be part of the perfect current—there's no need to push the river; let the river guide *you*. Less is more.

The Yoga of the Voice invites harmony practices, particu-larly when it's time to clear clouds of excessive information. It's good to meet the breath and listen to the breath-made sound of others when it's time to collaborate and exchange musical energy among people, and between heaven and earth. In har-mony, we are never alone.

exercise 40 Harmony Among Neighbors: A Magic Recipe

Go outdoors to your porch or window, fill your face with sun-light, and accompany the lively feeling by singing a long tone. Let the tone be sustained enough to become one with the beam of light. When your voice is as enlightened as your tone, invite your next-door neighbor to share the music by singing another long tone on a different pitch at the same time. Stand next to each other, elbow to elbow, or back to back. Listen to your neighbor. Make your duet last as long as possible by singing different notes at the same time, with silent pauses in between. You are the maestro, conducting the entry and the exit of tone and breath. Repeat this practice in the evening using the natural harmony of the crickets as a drone in the background. You are listening to the most precise harmony of the planet, and your neighbor will probably love you forever.

The Harmonic Humming Choir

▶ Listen to track 28: Harmonic Humming Choir

In cultivating the art of improvisation, one of my favorite practices goes like this: get a group to stand close to each other, creating a configuration I like to call an "acoustic egg." Some participants stand in the center with the others around them in the circle. Everyone can easily hear each other. I remind participants to listen carefully to their neighbors as we share a very soft humming in unison—so soft it is hard to hear. We do that twice. Then I ask the group to gradually hum a bit louder, still in unison. Eventually, I invite them to depart from that one-sound hum and sing a different tone, at the same time: we are harmonizing, starting very softy, and gradually getting louder.

Eventually, this amazing resonant choir will reach a peak; everyone has goose bumps. Almost magically, the group—as a single organism—experiences the spontaneous desire to dissolve into silence. This marks the end of the practice. All the secret frequencies of the universe have been set free. (It's not a bad idea to have a little bell on hand to mark the ending if time is a consideration. People become so absorbed that this exercise can last for an hour or two.)

This phenomenon reminds me of these words from Karlheinz Stockhausen, one of the most sophisticated composers of the twentieth century: "Set sail for the sun. Play a tone for so long until you hear its individual vibrations. Hold the tone and listen to the tones of others—to all of them together, not to the individual ones—and slowly move your tone until you arrive at complete harmony and the whole sound turns to gold, to pure shimmering fire."[7]

RHYTHM: MEASURABLE MUSIC

Rhythm and the universe were born on the same day. There is a "before" and there is an "after." There is a silence in between, and we perceive time only in relation to a phenomenon or a process on which time is projected. If there is no change, then the mind cannot conceive of time. So, we experience time when we experience change.

Messiaen writes, "Rhythm is first and foremost the change of number and duration. Suppose that there were a single beat in all the universe. One beat; with eternity before it and eternity after it. A before and an after. That is the birth of time. Imagine then, almost immediately, a second beat. Since any beat is prolonged by the silence which follows it, the second beat will be longer than the first. Another number, another duration. That is the birth of Rhythm."[8]

Rhythm is time, and music is (loosely) organized sound in time. We experience music as duration in time that can be measured and ordered. Rhythm organizes the movement of time in music. Plato applied the term *rhythm* to the order in that movement. Everything that lives moves in rhythm: all matter is vibration, and vibration moves in rhythm, hence *we* are rhythm. Rhythm is inherent to our nature as vibrational energy beings. Singing, therefore, is a vehicle through which we connect to every pulse of life itself, a vehicle fueled by our own breath and longing—a vehicle so eco-friendly that it leaves no harmful emissions.

exercise 41 Rhythmic Vitamins:
Another Magic Recipe

Go to your medicine cabinet and pick up two bottles of vitamins or pills. Find a quiet place, and hold one bottle in each hand. Create a slow, steady beat with the bottle in your left hand. With the bottle in your right hand, triple that beat—so that your left hand is shaking one beat while the right shakes three. Give a strong accent to the beat in the left hand. Start at a medium tempo, and don't speed up. Continue until it becomes natural.

After a few minutes, start playing a bit faster. Make those pills sound like dancing a waltz with the stars. When you are ready and in the groove, accompany the left-hand beat with a vocal sound like *toc*. You have just discovered the magic vitamin of polyrhythms.

Why is rhythm essential to music? Its function is to distribute sound and silence according to the demands of the melody in the musical space. The three basic modes of temporal organization are pulse, meter, and rhythm.

Pulse. Like ticks of a watch, pulses mark off equal units (or beats) in the temporal continuum. Pulse is necessary for the existence of meter and (usually) underlies and reinforces a rhythmic experience. Pulse is a great point of entry for music improvisation, especially when we connect the pulse with the body's pulses and "embody" it by playing it with a foot, or perhaps the hands, or the fingers. But we don't have to confine the pulse to our hands or feet. My Brazilian-informed body naturally expresses the pulse first with my dancing shoulders, and then my entrained Indian-music brain begins to mark the beat with my head.

Meter. We can understand meter as the measurement of pulses between accents that occur with some regularity. When we count pulses in this metric context, we refer to them as beats. For meter to exist, some of the pulses in the series must be accented—marked for emphasis—relative to others. The accented beats are called "strong" and the unaccented beats are called "weak." In this context, rhythm may be defined as the way in which one or more unaccented beats are grouped in relation to an accented one; thus, rhythm can be independent of meter, but it usually has a pulse as a foundation. Beats are pulses; rhythms are groupings.

Rhythm. Musical rhythm, like poetic rhythm, can also be free rhythm that it is not confined to keeping fixed time. Here, time is left to the sensibility of the interpreter, who creates a particular musical universe where the intervals between sounds and silence are charged with an emotional weight, a particular tonal density, and shifting dynamics.

Singing and clapping are the most enjoyable (and precise) modalities for learning and capturing the vitality inherent in the experience of rhythm. Nothing is more here and now. While melody and harmony are essential musical phenomena, rhythm is universal because it is perceived in all manifestations of life.

DURATION

Not one sound fears the silence that
extinguishes it. And no silence exists that is not
pregnant with sound.
JOHN CAGE, *Lecture on Something*

For years, I watched my students struggle with rhythm during our Yoga of the Voice, music, or raga practices. It became a special mission of mine to find ways to make the experience of rhythm more playful and accessible for everyone (and for myself). On a happy day, while completely absorbed in analyzing the musical language of the fantastic composer, Olivier Messiaen, I encountered his notion of rhythm as arising from an extension of *duration* in time rather than from a *division* of time. What matters is the length, how long something lasts. I realized that the concept of duration—which is inherent to the mathematical concept of rhythm—was much friendlier than that of division, and encourages people to experience rhythm in a more natural and creative way.

The first step is to deconstruct rhythm—playing long sustained notes, playing with pace and the space in between, inviting as many pauses and as much silence as possible, with slow melodies, and long-held notes or chords inducing a meditative mood. Afterward, you can play shorter tones, anticipating movement and more action, and then you can start tapping a steady pulse with a hand (or foot), playing your body as you would a drum. Now the focus has shifted from the long notes and is totally on the pulse (equal tapping).

Get involved with the equal beat, maybe grooving with your head and singing *sha* to every tap (beat). Get used to the groove. Embody the groove. Then do some taps *without* your voice— keep tapping steadily, but voice the beat randomly, and you'll notice that after a while there is only your voice, your tapping, and the beat. Nothing else exists.

You are making serious, *measurable* music. Eventually, you can add dynamics of volume, and more timbre. If you get lost, remember that you can return again and again to the experience of duration—the space between short and long length of time. A mystic would say that duration feels like the longing of rhythm for space.

Rhythm is the moving ground where tone meets time, and through the sense of duration we can experience rhythm as the arrangement of durable sounds, as an alternative to counting the beats. There is a correlation of two factors: one is time and the other is the grouping of notes in patterns created by the motion of tones (rhythm). Thus, the rhythmic life of a piece of music rests on the continuous interplay of duration, pattern, and silence. It is the combined experience of time and timelessness. You, the human factor, spice it up with feeling.

Nature's Pulse

Everything starts with vibration and pulse, and a pulse is the easiest way to start a rhythm. Pulse can be very, very fast. When we play the pulse sufficiently fast, the progressive acceleration causes us to hear the pulse as one long tone. What's more amazing is that we can actually *see* this. A computer can make an acoustical representation of singing or playing, called a sonogram, where each beat shows up as a distinct sound wave. As the pulse gets faster and faster, the wave line flattens and appears as a straight line—the identity of one long tone.

Pulse is periodic, sound timed by equal space, like a clock ticking or rhythms of a healthy body. An example of equal pulse is the shaman's drum that plays a steady beat to awaken the messengers of the spirit world. Shamanic drumming and rattling are a favorite practice for many who hear the fascinating call of the spirit world.

When we get familiar with different pulses, we can break the rules again, and learn to distinguish periodicity from non-periodicity. These contrasting concepts were the lightning bolt that helped my musical brain to play in time, and I became a natural percussionist.

Non-periodicity, or aperiodicity, is intrinsic to the music of nature: birdsong, ocean waves, the movement of wind and rain. We can find the same delight we experience in nature's music by performing non-periodical pulses and rhythms creatively. It is the art of non-repetition, combined with parts of steady pulses, that actually facilitates our concentration. According to the Gestalt Principles of perception, contrast is the appreciation of differences. The more we allow for noise and non-periodical movement of time, the more our brain will appreciate orderly sound and metered music. As we go in and out of pulse, we become more aware of the nature of change. Music unfolds through changes of.time.

One of my all-time favorite practices is singing vocables (syllables with vowels and consonants but no meaning) non-periodically, with no time or meter, with free rhythm and open pulse, using any sound, any vocal "noise," or any tone, as long as I want to. We can combine this free rhythm with repetition of vocables in a steady pulse. The amazing effective quality of this practice depends on continuity—doing it non-stop for at least two or three minutes. My name for this practice is *vocality*—it sounds like gibberish, but it has the intention of refreshing our musical mind and tapping into the core of creative expression, while it cunningly prepares our brain for more confined music.

Among its benefits, the practice of non-periodic singing opens our minds and musical frontiers, and it increases our capacity to listen to and understand the creativity in the great contemporary music of the twentieth and twenty-first centuries. I also encourage the practice of drum language (for example, singing in eight beats on the sounds: *takita taka taka.* You can hear a demonstration of drum language on the accompanying audio, which I encourage you to accompany with movement. This vitalizes our experience of rhythm and improves the kinesthetic coordination between movement and voice. Sing your beat!

▷ Listen to track 29: Drum Language

Sung rhythms can be a powerful spiritual practice. The use of rhythmic chanting to induce changes in consciousness is common in traditional cultures, where people use music with short, repeated phrases and a hypnotic beat so that time seems to slow or stop. Practices that encourage a combination of non-periodical rhythmic passages and the continuity of a steady beat transcend the sense of real-time progression, so that we live in mythological rather than chronological time. The drum and the voice are the natural vehicles for this transformational psychic journey in which time becomes timeless.

RAGA

I am delighted to introduce you to what I believe is the most exquisite form of musical expression—the art of raga singing. In the classes and workshops I teach, our practice almost always takes us into the royal realm of raga. Many of my students are advancing into the study of the ragas—they consider it the quintessence of their Yoga of the Voice practice. It's easy to get captivated by this ancient vocal art. We always want more.

Ragas are the essence of Indian classical music, and the voice is the most esteemed instrument for expressing them. On the simplest level, a raga is an ancient tonal arrangement conveyed through a series of three to seven notes belonging to a particular *that* (or scale), which is governed by specific rules for ascending and descending patterns and microtonal ornamentation.

Indian music virtuoso and composer Ravi Shankar describes raga in more detail:

> A raga is a scientific, precise, subtle and aesthetic melodic form with its own peculiar ascending and descending movement consisting of either a full seven note octave, or a series of six or five notes (or a combination of any of these) in a rising or falling structure . . . It is the subtle difference in the order of notes, an omission of a dissonant note, an emphasis on a particular note, the slide from one note to another, and the use of microtones together with other subtleties, that demarcate one raga from the other.[9]

It is said that human beings did not create the ragas. Ragas are like visitors, the artistic manifestation of *ghandarvas,* celestial beings known for their superb musical skills. Ragas are gifts to humans and transmit spiritual information, passion, and healing from these divine beings through the medium of melody.

I studied for twenty-eight years at the feet of maestro Ali Akbar Khan (1922–2009), regarded as the most illustrious contemporary figure in North Indian classical music. Khan is acclaimed worldwide for his luminous compositions and renowned as a performer for "playing like a lion," as beautifully documented in a recent film by the same name. (See the resources section.) The late concert violinist Lord Yehudi Menuhin proclaimed Ali Akbar Khan "an absolute genius . . . the greatest musician in the world."[10] Yet the maestro rarely claimed to have composed a raga. He *received* ragas. I recall some classes where we would sit for a very long time while warming up our instruments and tuning our voices with the sargam, up and down, until finally Khansahib would say, almost in a whisper, "Class is over, the raga didn't come today."

Encountering and being receptive to the ragas has elevated my appreciation of music. The ragas spring from a divine source, and we have to be respectful, tune in, and receive them. Their selfless essence teaches us not just how to sing or play, but how to nurture a spiritual practice.

The ghandarvas who supposedly send the ragas to us are supernatural sky dancers, so ragas are intimately connected with the natural and supernatural worlds. Each raga is associated with a certain time of day, season, quality of light, color, divinity, and other attributes. There are ragas that have the magical power to bring rain or fire; others pay homage to the moon. If you are familiar with these attributes, it is most beneficial to practice the ragas at the appropriate times. It's not uncommon to find yourself with a headache if you try to sing an energizing morning raga late in the evening when your body is getting ready for bed. (However, Khansahib would say that if you don't know the actual time a raga is supposed to be played, it's not going to affect your system. Ragas were not made to hurt us.)

The word *raga* is derived from a Sanskrit root meaning "to color, to dye." Figuratively, it evokes the qualities of passion, love, desire, and delight, particularly when applied to music or singing. The term as we know it first came into use in a classical Sanskrit treatise on music (dated between the fifth and eighth centuries) that describes raga as a combination of tones which, with beautiful illuminating grace, colors the mind with an emotion. Another inspired passage implies that ragas are melodic entities that live at the threshold between passion and music, humanness and cosmic-ness, religion and paganism, the sacred and the profane, sound and consciousness.

How can we define in a few words a simple melody that has so many extra-musical meanings? Its development through rules and patterns of ascending and descending notes and circular microtonal movement inspires a melodic development that is as complex as a symphony and as on-the-spot as jazz improvisation. At the same time, a raga is so free and also so effective in shifting the mood of all people. When a raga is playing, it's impossible not to be affected by it—even if you aren't particularly attuned to it, or you know nothing about the music.

It's possible that ragas represent the first structured psycho-acoustic music ever conceived. In his book, *Hindustani Music: A Tradition in Transition,* author Deepak S. Raja claims that "Raga is a psycho-acoustic hypothesis, which states that melody, created and rendered in accordance with a certain set of rules, has a high probability of eliciting a certain quality of emotional response."[11]

Raja goes on to explain, "As a melodic entity, a Raga . . . is represented by a set of rules governing the selection, sequencing, and treatment of tones/*swara-s*. These rules define a framework, which is tight enough to ensure aesthetic coherence, while also providing sufficient freedom for individual creativity."[12] This approach comes from a tradition that combines the role of the composer, the performer, and the deity in the same individual.

To me, a raga is a melodic narration with the power to induce deep emotional clearing and a sensitive aliveness rooted in beauty. This is why my students always seem to want more of it, even though ragas require a lot of practice, repetition, and, as much as possible in the beginning, a direct connection with a live teacher—until the raga itself becomes the teacher. Learning the ragas is like learning a new language. Even if we didn't grow up hearing the nuances of these sounds, there is a wide range of complementary practices that allow us to become more sensitive to the language of raga.

The Yoga of the Voice assists students in recognizing the particular tonal patterns and becoming familiar with the heart melodies of the ragas. I like to identify these patterns as the "passport" to the raga. Recognition of these patterns offers students a playful frame of reference for interacting with the potential of each raga and for creating more music. Practices that involve deep listening, tuning with the sargam, singing with a drone, Nada Yoga, slow dhrupad syllables, and vocal meditation take us right to the doorstep of raga. My inspired collaborator, John Beaulieu, founder of BioSonics Enterprises, worked with me to develop a set of raga tuning forks. Using these forks, which are tuned to each of the thirteen notes of the octave, a person can listen with the whole body and hear "inside" the intervals and within the srutis. Yoga of the Voice students have enthusiastically embraced this new technology, which allows them to fine-tune their auditory perception of the intervals.

Conceived as a yoga practice, the ragas offer a direct experience of singing as a healing art. Singing the ragas awakens higher levels of appreciation, where the sacred becomes commonplace and music touches a source beyond ordinary listening. The poised architecture hidden in the raga moves us toward a transpersonal sense of self that's free from the poverty of the ego. We are immersed in the unfolding of an ancient melody that evokes archetypal consciousness. We are inside a prayer.

We are also outside of time. In "The Predicament of Raga Music," Raghava R. Menon writes: "The hidden agenda of Indian classical music has always been spiritual . . . [it] has no truck with history or man's passage through time. Yesterday and today is the same for the music of the raga. It only accepts the leading edge of now as its principal concern . . . This non-historical quality, this built-in timelessness and autonomy in the core of its still centre, is achieved by a highly resolute use of the voice as its substance."[13]

The melodic approach we find in the ragas might not be unique to Indian classical music. When musicians of varied backgrounds attain a certain level of genius and the spirits call, the musicians begin longing for the ragas—and the ragas come to them, whether they know them by name or not. We find raga within the saxophone solos of John Coltrane and in the compositions of George Harrison, both of whom studied the ragas. It also appears in the music of Egberto Gismonti and Astor Piazzolla. It also appears in Mahler's adagio movements, Bach's cello suites, and Mozart's piano concertos in which one heart melody becomes the seed of monumental music.

When I first encountered these musical entities—the ragas—I found my spiritual practice, my temple, my teacher, and my true nature as a humble musician in quest of reenchanting the world. I immediately fell in love with the creative potential of these divine melodies. We are making art with each movement of tone to tone in a delicate balance between organization and fantasy.

A wealth of resources for listening to, practicing with, and reading more about the ragas is available in the resources section at the end of the book.

RASA

Through music, one can reach God.
RAVI SHANKAR

Raga cannot be considered separately from its counterpart, *rasa*. If raga is that which colors the mind with emotion, rasa *is* the emotion, the experience of that color, and the "tasting" of the mood conveyed by the tones of the raga. If raga is a garland of flowers, then rasa is the perfume of the flower, the delicate essence of a fruit. Rasa is an essential part of India's theory of art. It speaks of the pure delight we feel when we encounter a work of art—the kind of bliss that can be experienced only by the spirit, which Indian treatises refer to as the "taste of the mind." Khansahib would say, "If there is no rasa when singing a raga, there is no more raga."

We can explore the meaning of rasa through words such as *taste, relish,* or *essence.* Like perfume, rasa isn't easy to describe, because its effect comes from non-physical properties rather than the physical matter from which it derives. In Indian alchemy, rasa is related to the essence of mercury, whose principal alchemical attribute is awareness.

In music listening, rasa conveys the idea of an aesthetic emotion to be tasted, knowable only in the activity of sensing. It exists only to the degree that it *has been* relished by the *rasika*, the hearer, and it compels an act of communion. Rasa does not belong to the work of art, the musician, or the listener, but it unites them all in the same state of consciousness and delight. In the Vedas, the experience of rasa is described as a flash of super-worldly blinding light that appears to those for whom the knowledge of ideal beauty is innate and intuitive.

In music practice, we can distinguish ten principal rasas that convey the emotional nature of the ragas.

Shringar: eroticism, passion, divine sensuality

Karuna: pathos, sadness, psychic pain, loss

Hasya: mirth, laughter, joy, celebration

Vira: heroism, courage, valor

Adbhuta: wonder, surprise, the fantastic

Shanti: peace, inner serenity

Tyag: renunciation, detachment, a cause for liberation

Bhakti: devotion

Gambhir: solemnity, seriousness

Chanchal: restlessness, playfulness

Rasa leads us to an in-depth exploration of the connection between emotion and music. Sentiments conveyed by music have not been given a lot of attention in Western musical education, captivated as it is by the accumulation of intellectual knowledge. The appreciation of rasa allows us to experience the most profound emotions. The mind experiences conscious joy even in the representation of painful events because of the integration of perceptual, emotional, and cognitive faculties, refined by subtle aesthetic dimensions of sensing, feeling, and listening.

The understanding of the concept of rasa is key to the healing potential of music. When we release emotion, we free ourselves from mental burdens. While singing or listening to music infused with rasa, our emotions appear like a cloud in the sky that dissolves into emptiness.

You will be interested to know that a continuing practice and study of the system of raga/rasa improves the ability to realize the emotional quality of a conflict we desire to resolve. If this happens, we may continue to generate a broader, more universal, less egoistic sense of well-being, and a brighter ear for great music and its power to release stress and lessen suffering in all our relationships.

Through singing the ragas (and mantras, invocations, prayers, or any song), the conscious experience of rasa trains the ear and the imagination. Understanding rasa also enhances the quality of our voice, inspiring us to explore more deeply the interdependence between timbre, tonality, sound, harmonic progression, duration, inner pulse, and the way that these musical elements affect consciousness.

Rasa evolves and changes with the movement of melody. In the chant form of *kirtan* (repetitive call-and-response chanting performed in India's devotional traditions), the chanting—if trustfully and tunefully performed—conveys devotion, joy, and peace. The ragas in their melodic grandeur may also render more than one rasa in their development; they might start with pathos, move to devotion, then joy, then detachment, then serenity, all unintentionally conveyed by the complete absorption of the singer in the music.

At the end of a Yoga of the Voice retreat when I ask the participants, "What are you taking home that can change your life and re-enchant the world?" most of them effusively reply: "Rasa!"

COSMIC MUSIC: MEDICINE MELODIES

In the universe, everything sings: plants, animals, waterfalls, bones, people, the stars, the rain, and many things we don't see. As I emphasize in this book, even silence makes a sound. From time immemorial, the shaman has heard the hidden music of the universe and sung it back through what I like to introduce as "medicine melodies," simple tonal configurations that reflect a sacred unity with nature and have the power to heal body, mind, and spirit. Many people today are *visited* by such melodies—as if spontaneous transmissions from nature or the spirit world are "singing into" the person rather than the person "singing out."

Almost every week, someone reaches out to me with a request like this: "I am not a singer, but I hear this beautiful music inside me, and sometimes when I can express that music it sounds like short and repetitive melodies, inspired by some spiritual presence, like someone is singing through me, and my voice sounds so free and open. Can you help me?" I always wonder why these gifted people are so worried—the singing feels like an incantation! It is a gift. It's a medicine melody born out of a spiritual connection.

What is extraordinary is that the music delivered by these melodies has the intention to assist, to lessen fear, to orient, to *abrir caminhos* (to open the way). Many cultures program us to think that the main purpose of music is entertainment. These melodies, on the other hand, are intuitive medicine. Singing them is an act of spontaneous reverence for a subtler dimension of reality, where we obtain spiritual information in a process I call *musical divination:* The music is in the air; by deep listening we are open to receive it. The mind has access to a higher realm where a medicine melody is heard. The voice is the gatekeeper. Spirit uses our voice as a vehicle to sing through us.

We can look at medicine melodies as healing-vibrational formulas that help transform energy patterns and enhance deep listening and receptivity. By balancing the activity of the left- and right-brain hemispheres, medicine melodies can produce measurable effects in the physical body. Singing or listening to them induces concentration and sharpens our capacity for self-awareness, allowing us to see not only what is there, but also what is felt, and what others feel, giving us access to an insightful vision of the past, present, and future.

Evoking the original function of music—which is to quiet the mind and make it sensitive to divine intervention—these archetypal melodies clear and open energetic channels. The simple contour of the melodies creates a contagious sensation of ancestral communion and well-being. Anyone who cultivates familiarity with chanting can find herself creating or remembering medicine melodies. It requires simply the ability to be completely present in the moment, allowing yourself to be subtly immersed in a transpersonal field of sound and fear-lessness—the mind of the shaman.

As sacred sound, a medicine melody travels through consciousness; it can transform everyday occurrences into a visionary dimension. A fundamental part of shamanic healing, medicine melodies possess profound consciousness-altering effects. Examples from the Peruvian Amazon are icaros, (as heard on audio track 24) songs that plants "transmit" to the healers as soon as they become physically, mentally, and spiritually prepared to receive the songs. After shamanic initiation, individuals in completely different locations have been known to receive the very same icaros—evidence of their direct transmission from sacred realms.

A shaman will sing medicine melodies for divination—obtaining information from the spirit world—and protection in support of the inner journey. The sacro-magical and transformative qualities of these chants make them central to medicine ritual. The practice involves using evocative voices that imitate nature and spirit sounds, simple chants, and deep drumbeats to facilitate the transference of energy and connect with the healing power of the elements of nature and the spirit world.

Some of the psycho-spiritual qualities (or rasas) that may be conveyed when people sing medicine melodies include inner wisdom, serenity, open-mindedness, selflessness, compassion, devotion, calm acceptance, wonder, affliction, detachment, inner joy, radiance, and relaxation. In music and sound therapy, both the clinician and patient can benefit from medicine melodies that generate an atmosphere of calm receptiveness.

Singing medicine melodies becomes a spiritual practice that involves both the body and mind, opening us to divine remembrance, nature, and transformation. The realm of sounding becomes a state of consciousness—a kind of trance—where the attention is not on the Self, but in the experience of listening. Free from selfish demands, the voice soars, listens, receives, and releases healing frequencies and songs. We wonder again, *Who is singing?*

Through medicine melodies, we become cosmic singers, connecting through sound to spirit, eternity, and light. Herein lies the beneficial power of this distinctive music that has no composer and no ownership, except for the intervention of the divine. In particular, we benefit by connecting with the archetypal dimension of consciousness and magic. Our hearts open to the deep longing of the enchanters, to those who journey through the magic of sound to attract spirit power.

So, there's nothing to worry about when you receive these melodies. You have been blessed. You have been listening to the voices of the unseen; you have tasted the "unseen fruit," described by the Sanskrit concept of *adrsta-phala* (spiritual benefit). Your voice is making cosmic music.

Spiritual Melodicism

Music involves a vital power of expression with inspiration coming from above . . . In its relation with sound, music can induce ecstatic trance as a form of spiritual intoxication, and through the practice of music, devotion and aspiration can grow and prepare one's nature for realization.

MIRRA ALFASSA, known in India as the "Supreme Mother"

In the beginning of this book, I presented my view on what I call musical materialism. Now is the right time to counter this with a more devotional alternative: spiritual melodicism. This concept encapsulates the conscious and elegant treatment of all the musical elements that we have been discussing—spiritually inspired melodies in perfect synergy with ethereal harmonies and rhythmic awareness abiding in time as duration—with a taste of rasa and a dash of cosmic energy. This spiritual treatment of music, inspired by the Eastern art of melody, conveys the language of intimacy, tells a story, and evokes meaning. In times of suffering and pain, the spiritual melodicism in your music will hold, embrace, and comfort, like an unconditionally loving mother.

Throughout human history, music has always been a source of spiritual nourishment, and the voice has been its most potent instrument. Spiritual melodicism taps into the primordial healing power of music. No matter how skillful a craftsman may be, no matter how sophisticated technology may become, no one ever has—or ever will—fashion a musical instrument more perfect than the human voice. It is humanity's most natural instrument, the closest to communicating divine resonance.

To benefit from the affective power of music, we attend to economy and mindful use of all musical components: melody, rhythm, mood, and harmony. We grow from deep listening to all sounds and all kinds of music, and from a conscious engagement with all aspects of the musical landscape. We cultivate the quality of tone in each breath. We develop the whole range of the voice, attending to the elements of volume, pace, texture, timbre, breath, placement, strength, articulation, and rasa. We nurture our sensibility through continuous practice and flow. What matters most is the transformation that follows.

BACK TO THE FOREST

Earlier in this chapter, we said that repetition, knowledge, collaboration, and music languages from other cultures can take our singing voice as far as we dream. We have the choice to go deeper into the architecture of music, learning more about scales, modes, the art of melody, and the mesmerizing ragas. We can choose to become masters of measurable music, to identify frequency ratios as friends, to know the values corresponding to each note, and to sing them in tune. We can even memorize all the intervals, read and write melodies fluently, deeply enjoy the intellectual dimension of music composition at large, and conduct our first symphony. We can also become interested in neuroscience and the effect of music on the brain and of the brain on music. It's all about how far the love for music will take us.

On the other hand, with no loss of beauty and vision, we can choose to get back to the forest and sing with the eternal shamans. We can make purely intuitive music—calling and responding to the songs of the birds and the roars of the jaguars. These spirited incantations have no numbers, no wrong notes, no mistakes. These voices precede us and are always available to us. The shamanic whispering is omnipresent. You are never alone. Like the Goddess in the mind, the shaman within us sings the inspired word in order to hear and heal.

Remember, you don't need to suffer to sing, you have to first feel free. Intuition is a way of perception—it makes beautiful music as well.

All you need is love.

9

Designing Your Practice

The more your music practice becomes regular,
the more real it feels and the more it pays off
. . . When you practice every day, you come into
resonance with cosmic cycles . . . The whole
spectrum of vibration, from the slow, lowest
tones of turning galaxies to the highest speeds
of inner light, becomes your musical realm.
W. A. MATHIEU, *The Listening Book*

If you're a reader who enjoys the reading more than
the doing—congratulations, your work is done! If you've been
looking forward to putting what you've been reading into practice, however, this section of the book is designed for you.

In chapter 2, we talked about how singing promotes health
and well-being. Throughout the rest of the book, we've shared
how a regular practice of singing as a yogi can enrich life even
more by:

enhancing concentration (*dharana*, the singleness of the mind on one point)

recognizing our own nature and condition, and how to abide in it (*rigpa*, the knowledge that arises from recognizing one's nature)

keeping the flow of energy open in the body and the mind (*Shakti*, the divine feminine creative power)

multiplying your connections (*Shiva*, the masculine principle that originates the multidimensional universe, and is immersed in complete and blissful union with Shakti)

cultivating devotional energy (*bhakti*, active involvement in the worship of the divine)

encouraging liberation from conditioning (*mukti*, the state of personal freedom and spiritual autonomy)

promoting purification of the mind (*shuddhi*, the state of clarity of the mind and personality)

clearing feelings to promote detachment (*vairagya*, the state of renunciation)

balancing what is out of balance (*samana*, sustaining a state of balance)

bringing inner serenity (*shanti*, attaining a state of calm and bliss)

Practice is an act of integration. We put together what was separated and connect with an inner guidance—the teacher within—from whom we get knowledge and who tells us that it's okay not to know, okay to make mistakes, and that it's highly desirable to offer our practice to something greater than ourselves.

Your practice beckons you to be a master designer of twenty-one minutes of uninterrupted voice and silence. Find a sequence of practices that you like to do. Cultivate discipline and participation. Find the delicate balance between order and creative chaos. Infuse your practice with rasa. Let it be private and profound. Make a cup of tea called devotion and be innocent like a child.

I invite you to approach singing practice as *dharma art,* a state of mind I learned from the artist and pre-eminent teacher of Tibetan Buddhism, Chögyam Trungpa Rinpoche. Dharma art is a creative work that springs from the awakened meditative state and provides a vehicle to appreciate and express without any struggle or desire to achieve. In Chögyam Trungpa's treasured words:

> In art, as in life generally, we need to study
> our craft, develop our skills, and absorb
> the knowledge and insight passed down by
> tradition. But whether we have the attitude
> of a student who could still become more
> proficient in handling the materials, or the
> attitude of an accomplished master, when
> we are actually creating a work of art there
> is a sense of total confidence. Our message
> is simply one of appreciating the nature of
> things as they are and expressing it without
> any struggle of thoughts and fears. We
> give up aggression, both toward ourselves,
> that we have to make a special effort to
> impress people, and toward others, that we
> can put something over on them. Genuine
> art—dharma art—is simply the activity of
> nonaggression.[1]

Singing is the path and the yoga. If you stay patiently and actively on the path, it will take you where you want to go. The practice will make you feel good. At that point, invite others to join you.

Staying on the Path

How do we make sure to stay on the path? We do it by starting at the same place and ending at the same place every time we practice. And we do it again, and again, and again. Not changing the beginning or end of a set of practices ensures that inner and outer changes will follow.

The idea is to develop a sequence that makes you feel engaged and repeat it until it feels like repeating a mantra. The 108 Strategies for Vocal Improvisation (on page 185) will give you inspiration and practical ideas for designing a routine you like. I recommend taking out a notebook and writing down a sequence of exercises that will become *your* practice, *your* path, at least for a while.

Beginning: You could start with a deep *ah,* an *Om,* or by listening to a drone and singing *ah* in unison with it, matching the tone. It's also very powerful to start by reading a short poem or highlights from your teacher's teachings or listening to his or her musical recordings. Follow this beginning with a few of the preliminary practices suggested in the 108 Strategies to connect with the breath and warm up the voice. You are creating a container and an orderly sequence.

Development: This is the middle section of your practice. Select a focus for each time you practice. Unfasten your creative intuition and be as outrageous as you wish when choosing your focus. The intention is to challenge yourself—without the tension of having to achieve something—and to investigate, to go deeper, to memorize, and to build on the skills you're learning. Some examples of focus are: flexible spine/flexible voice, the magic of tone and the shape of the lips, tuning and duration, listening to breath becoming tone, or any combination of the 108 Strategies on page 185.

Ending: When you have finished your practice, give yourself any sound and posture that will help you relax and integrate— such as an *Om,* or a mantra from any culture, or simply five minutes of silent meditation. Repeat the same ending every time you practice. Create an ending that is relaxing and that conveys reverence for space as a well-deserved reminder that you are on the path. It's like dessert after the perfect meal.

We want to bring into our practice the spaciousness of meditation. As the practice becomes more familiar, the voice becomes freer and more fluid—and we feel more musical free-dom as well. With freedom comes more confidence in our voice. Confidence strengthens manifestation, and manifestation makes for fulfillment. This is the kind of experience that makes you a practitioner, and it never stops unfolding.

Here are a few helpful things to keep in mind when you practice:

Follow your voice.

Your voice is an offering.

Music and singing are about listening.

Meet and listen to your breath before singing.

Sound follows breath and breath follows sound.

A flexible spine makes a flexible voice.

Subtle movements of the spine, hands, and arms benefit voice production.

The hands follow the voice and the voice follows the hands.

Duration transcends the limitations of time—lengthen your tones.

Benefits multiply with uninterrupted vocal exercises performed for at least twenty-one minutes.

Confidence develops through cultivating familiarity.

Repetition is your friend.

The devotional mind is a result of "dwelling" in a disciplined practice.

When the music of your voice slows down, you are listening.

Less is more.

There is something in music beyond ordinary listening.

Silence is your best friend.

If possible, start your practice at the same time and place each day. You are creating a very private sanctuary for your body and voice. Give yourself at least three months of practice so that you can cultivate familiarity with the voice as your ally and your friend—and relish the fullness of your voice.

Keep it up. Don't give up the path.

POINTS OF ENTRY

> *The journey of a thousand miles begins*
> *with a single step.*
> LAO TZU

Points of entry are creative strategies that we employ to trigger the process of making music. They're very useful in our daily practice but especially important when we decide to play with others.

Once we embark on the journey of music-making, most of us find it easy to continue and to enjoy the sonic adventures as they unfold. Taking the first step, however, or even knowing which direction to face before taking that first step, can be the most delicate part of any journey because we might feel our vulnerability and find ourselves having to walk through fears, doubts, and tensions to make the right choices. It's good to be conscious of all of these, but be gentle with both the feelings and the self. It might be necessary to make a leap of faith and to surrender fully to the moment and to the music to come. The life of a serious music creator is about making aural choices—there is always a creative risk in all beginnings and endings.

A point of entry is the first step on the audacious journey of music making. For example, to start a car we need a key. In fact, first we need the key to open the car door so that we can get in; then we need the key to start the engine. When the engine turns over, we know we're ready for the road. A point of entry gives us the precise turn of the key we need to drive into a sound expedition.

Simply put, a point of entry is the practice we select to open our first door, to unlock the body of the voice, to ignite our creative imagination, and to begin our musical journey. The selection of keys available to us is immensely diverse, drawn from many old and new traditions as well as from an unlimited number of variations that each practitioner might discover according to a particular situation and mood.

Here's an example of how I used a particular point of entry at an evening of interactive music for a group of 250 people in the country of Estonia. I didn't know a single person. We were savoring two minutes of silence following an hour of transcendent call-and-response chanting. After a devotional experience like that, I often ask for comments or questions. This helps people transition from the delicate, subtle state of consciousness we've opened into a more ordinary state of relating. On this occasion, after very long consideration, someone from the group asked simply, "How do you start?"

On this particular evening, I had decided to begin on a playful note as a way of expressing my appreciation and surprise for all the people who showed up without knowing a thing about me or about my work. So I started with a creative inquiry. "Why do you think I came here—all the way from California to Estonia— to be in this room with you?" I asked several times while moving around the room in order to feel closer to the audience. Nobody replied, but they all were guessing. Then I said, "Because I fell in love with the name of my host, *Alar*, and with all the other Estonian names I heard." Shortly after, I sang "Alar," and before we knew it, 250 people were merrily singing their names with on-the-spot improvised melodies. It was glorious!

With this lighthearted opening of the voice and heart—which playfully revealed the personalities of former strangers—we easily shifted into a more sophisticated musical dimension by means of call-and-response devotional singing. Together we were creating a universal sacred space through sound. We were on the path of the Yoga of the Voice. I was home in Estonia, and we were all inhabitants of Planet Music.

We always start where everything begins—in silence. In this silence, we assess the state of things: the mood, the energy, the psychoacoustics of the room, and, just as important, our own state of being, mood, and vibrational field. It only takes a moment. With practice, the business of making the unfamiliar familiar becomes second nature.

In the process, we awaken to the symptoms of spontaneous resonance. On that evening in Estonia, my assessment began with an inquiry into my own state of being: "Why am I here?" Because I like the music of Estonian names. What a wonderful thing to share with the people of Estonia. That led us all to share the same truthful moment, which led to a creative improvisation. The "singing of the names" was the key: our point-of-entry practice.

In this situation, my extended experience as a Gestalt psychotherapist paid off. By being in the here and now, letting it unfold and flow, and staying present at every moment, I guided the group to a simple and powerful experience.

Espressivo/Contemplativo

When considering a point of entry, we can either take the outgoing road of open expression: *espressivo* (as I did with the Estonians) or the more inward road of contemplative creativity: *contemplativo*. These choices are always available whether we are singing by ourselves or with a group.

On the expressive route, the practices are outgoing and external. The Open Sound practice in chapter 1 (see page 8) is a good example of the expressive modality. Contemplative practices tend to be slower, quieter, and more inward. We are listening to our internal sound. Practices of listening to the breath and lengthening tone are examples of the contemplative mode.

We choose our direction by paying attention to our intention and the conditions here and now. The rest is a delicate balance between intuition and knowledge of musical components.

When we invite others to enter the musical space with us in this way, resonance and entrainment happen. There is no resistance, but flow, and we begin moving and singing together at the same frequency.

We can draw from a large range of practices (see the 108 Strategies for Vocal Improvisation on page 185). What's important is to settle on a way to enter the improvisation and to have a sense of how to exit when you've reached the end. With those two key points established in your mind, you have the freedom and the confidence to jump into the musical unknown.

Listen carefully, and don't be surprised if sometimes the voice and the music you have chosen as the point of entry become an amazing composition in itself. It is usually the case.

108 Strategies of Vocal Improvisation

Over the years, the many groups I've worked with have inspired me to develop strategies for improvising with the voice and to expand the practice of the Yoga of the Voice. The following list offers some of these strategies. Use them as guidance and let them be a springboard for your creative imagination.

PRELIMINARY PRACTICES

Always begin your practice with awareness of posture. Stand or sit with your weight comfortably balanced on the four corners of your feet, shoulders relaxed, hands open and empty, chin parallel to the floor, and eyes soft.

Breath
Select at least three practices for connecting with breath to begin your practice.

1. Aware Breathing Practices: See chapter 7, page 106.

2. In and Out Breathing in Three Parts: Inhale slowly and deeply, hold for a count of five, exhale long.

3. Hands as Clouds: See chapter 5, page 71.

4. Neck Circles: Holding the breath in the belly, very slowly rotate the neck in a complete circle five times clockwise and five times counterclockwise. Keep your eyes open. At the end, exhale upward toward the crown while lifting your arms overhead (optional). Lower your arms and rest in fresh awareness.

5. Long Straw: See chapter 7, page 107.

6. Inner Fire: With relaxed shoulders, bend at the waist with your hands on your belly or on your knees. Inhale and exhale rapidly through your nose five times. Keep your eyes open and rest in fresh awareness after the practice.

7. Blowing: Softly, steadily, and slowly blow. Try different lip openings with each new breath.

8. Ball of Light: See chapter 5, page 67.

Consciousness: Sound Meditations
These sound meditations engage our capacity for deep listening and allow the mind to become spacious and clear. These practices are all inspired by my mentor and friend, Pauline Oliveros. (See the resources section to learn where to find more sonic meditations from Pauline.)

9. Breath as Sound: Observe your own breathing, gradually allowing it to become audible. Play with the many sounds of the breath.

10. Deep Listening: Focus on sounds near and far and on the silence between each layer of sound. (See Unstruck Sound practice, chapter 6, page 91.)

11. Telepathic Resonance: In a dyad or a group, imagine the sound that another person may be listening to. Using your voice and/or your body, make audible the sound that you imagine.

12. Phonetic Awareness: Dissect your name, vocally exploring the sound of each letter and each syllable. Let those sounds make music.

13. Silent Recitation of a Mantra: Chose a mantra or any meaningful phrase, listen to the vibration of it, and recite it silently. (See "Mantra Practices," chapter 7, page 126.)

14. Listening to Your Lover: Imagine your beloved calling you on the phone. Listen inwardly to the texture of his or her voice and use your voice to make the quality of tone you are hearing audible.

Warm-Ups: Activating the Body of the Voice
These practices are great for waking up the voice and body on the espressivo path.

15. Open Sound/Any Sound: See chapter 1, page 8.

16. Calls, Cries, and Clamors: This is a great practice to project the power of your voice. Calls are aimed at potential listeners, especially a divine listener, and they can take the form of a prayer or supplication. Cries can express sadness or astonishment, and they can become a clamor when made by a group. Wail, exult, moan, go wild—but don't strain your instrument.

17. High-Pitched One-Sound Invocation: Call in a deity or a quality you desire using only one note or type of sound. Listen to track 30: High-Pitched One-Sound Invocation.

18. Humming: Hum softly with closed lips to produce a long and relaxed sound whenever you feel like restarting your paractice or reconnecting with the here and now.

19. Mumming: This is like humming, but you use the syllable *mum* repeated on a monotone. Feel how the sound resonates in the forehead and along the entire spine.

20. Scanning: See the Recharging the Brain practice in chapter 2, page 30.

21. Bullroarer: See the Recharging the Brain practice in chapter 2, page 30.

22. Animal Calls: Play with all varieties of animal calls, both soft and loud.

23. Kecak Voices: Imitate the voices (and movement) of the Balinese monkey chant. (You can easily find videos that demonstrate the monkey chant on the Internet.)

24. Inuit Games: Imitate the breathy sound of Inuit throat singing, with audible inhalations. (You can search the Internet to find video demonstrations of Inuit throat singing.)

25. Cauldron Warming: Using a low voice, stir up the sound of a cauldron in your belly.

26. Recitation/Monotone Voices with a Pulse: Imagine you are a monk (or many monks) chanting monotonously over a drum beat.

27. Sopro: See "Aware Breathing Practices" in chapter 7, page 106.

28. Motorcycle Mouth: While blowing through loose lips, go up and down the scale like a motorbike revving its engine. Listen to track 31: Motorcycle Mouth.

29. Bubble and Shake: With loose lips, create bubbling sounds while you shake your head.

30. Energetic *Ha* Breath: Imagining a marching band, move your arms energetically up and down with each exhalation on *ha*.

31. Inhaling with Sound: Apply the sounds of your inhalation to create a short repetitive pattern (*ostinato*). Remember to exhale as well—and keep your eyes open. Take refreshing breaths in between.

SONIC YOGIC PRACTICES

The following are practices that come from ancient yogic traditions.

Nada Yoga: Vibration, Sound, Consciousness

32. Silent *Om:* See chapter 6, page 89.

33. Unstruck Sound: See chapter 6, page 91.

34. The Music of Your Heart: Warm up your hands by rubbing them together. Then place them on your chest and softly tap the beat of your heart.

35. Sounding the Sound Within: See chapter 6, page 92.

36. Unbroken Sound: See chapter 6, page 94. Listen to audio track 10.

37. Prayer in Dhrupad (*Ananda Hari Om*): See chapter 6, page 96. Listen to audio track 11.

Shabda Yoga: Sacred Words, Seed Syllables, Mantras

38. Brahm, the Creator: See chapter 6, page 97. Listen to audio track 12.

39. Bija Syllables: See chapter 6, page 98. Listen to audio track 13.

40. Elemental Seed Sounds: See chapter 7, page 116. Listen to audio track 16.

41. Mantra (*Om Sree Amma Narayani Namastute*): See chapter 7, page 126. Listen to audio track 22.

Bhakti Yoga: Chants of Devotion

42. Chanting the Names: Call the name of deities of any tradition as an invocation.

43. Chanting to the Mother (*Jaya Ma*): Repetitively chant these words in a slow kirtan style.

44. Chant of Dedication (*Twameva Mata*): See chapter 7, page 132. Listen to audio track 25.

Tantra Yoga: Chants of Transformation

45. Chanting *Ah:* Focus on the heart chakra and imagine rainbow lights radiating from the heart.

46. Tara Mantra (*Om Tare Tutare Ture Swaha*): See Invocation Practices in chapter 7, page 126. Listen to audio track 17.

47. Tibetan Mantra (*Om Mani Padme Hum*): Bringing the vibration of *compassion* to your heart, repeat this mantra as many times as possible. See "Mantra Practices" in chapter 7, page 126. Listen to audio track 21.

48. Medicine Buddha Mantra (*Om Ma Hum*): Bringing the vibration of *healing* to your heart, repeat this mantra as many times as possible, coordinating breath with sound and sound with breath. See "Mantra Practices" in chapter 7, page 126.

TUNING THE VOICE

Tuning the voice is an essential part of a successful music practice. Try to incorporate at least one of these exercises into your routine.

49. Sargam (*Sa Re Ga Ma Pa Dha Ni Sa*): Sing up and down the sargam scale, slowly singing each note. Focus on the approach to each note, neighboring notes, microtones, and intervals. Slow is always better. See chapter 8, page 136.

50. Sargam Circles: Departing from each note, slide microtonally to the lower octave and return to the note you started from. As you circle with your voice, draw circles with your hand to direct the sound.

51. Singing Intervals with a Drone: With a drone accompaniment of any kind, sing any two-note intervals using the sargam syllables or just the syllable *ah*.

52. Sounding the Space in Between: Listening deeply, slowly explore the space between any two notes using microtonal bending tones.

VOCAL IMPROVISATION

There are unlimited avenues to vocal improvisation. Use these suggestions to fire up your creative imagination. Feel free to add your own improvisations and ways to participate.

The Contemplative Voice
Here are some great exercises on the path of the contemplativo.

53. Chanting *Ah:* Chant in many registers and with many textures.

54. Chanting *Sa:* Chant continuously, slowly dwelling on one tone (the tonic).

55. Toning: See chapter 7, page 111.

56. Overtone Singing: Curve the sides of the tongue upward touching the upper molars to create a cave in the mouth, intone the sound *errr* on a steady pitch, listening for the overtones and fine-tuning the harmonics with slight movements of the lips and the tongue.

57. Vocal Meditation: See chapter 7, page 123. Listen to audio track 20.

Spontaneous Song
The improvisation strategies below connect words and meaning to melody and rhythm. You are the composer and lyricist. Trust your pure intuition and follow the stream of your musical consciousness. See the example of "Self-Generated Prayer" in chapter 7, page 128.

58. Self-Generated Prayer

59. Self-Generated Poetry

60. Self-Generated Lullaby

61. Sing a Letter to Your Beloved

The Voices of the Voice: Who Is Singing?
Here's an opportunity to experiment with how much range and expression your voice can have. The following suggestions cover a wide territory of styles, modes, and dynamics, as well as variations on pitch, volume, texture, timbre, breath, placement, strength, articulation, and rasa. Use the suggested voices below as springboards for your creativity. Be open and inventive—there is no right or wrong. Just enjoy playing with different styles and feel free to create your own list of the voices of *your* voice.

62. Theatrical Voices

63. Operatic Voices

64. Jazzy Voices

65. Dancing Voices

66. Percussive Voices

67. Siren Voice

68. Indigenous Voices

69. Monastic Voices

70. Prayerful Voices

71. Whispering Voices

72. Spirit Voices

73. Children's Voices

74. Voice of the Elements: watery, earthy, fiery, airy, etheric

75. Voice of Plants

76. Voice of Insects

77. Voice of Liberation

78. Voice as Waves of Energy

79. Voice of the Goddess

Accompanied Voice
At any moment in your improvisation, you might want to include an instrument or to accompany yourself with movement. The key is to enhance your singing voice by exploring usual and unusual ways to accompany it. Focus on the approach and the connection.

80. Singing with a Drum

81. Singing with Shakers

82. Singing with Prerecorded Music

83. Singing with Tibetan Bowls or Bells

84. Singing with Water Sounds

85. Singing with Body Percussion

86. Voice with Mudra (hand/finger gestures)

87. Voice Unaccompanied

Vocal Forms and Styles
During your practice (particularly toward the end), you can rely on any vocal forms and styles that make you feel at home on Planet Music. These are all good practices to share in a group.

88. Inward Singing: See chapter 5, page 69. Listen to audio track 6.

89. Invocation: See "Invocation Practices" in chapter 7, page 119. Listen to audio tracks 17–19.

90. Medicine Melodies: Create your own short medicine melodies. See chapter 8, page 168.

91. Love Songs

92. Ballads

93. Hymns

94. Arias

95. Lamentations

96. Alleluias, Amens, and African-American Spirituals

97. Ragas

98. Yodeling: Sing in wide intervals, spanning low and high registers, without masking the breaks in the voice.

99. Singing a Favorite Song (as a way to introduce and create a new song.)

100. Singing a Children's Song

101. Harmony and Rounds: This is a good practice to do in a group.

102. Voice in Unison: This can be done in a group, with one other person, or by singing in unison with drones.

103. Voice Singing Very High and Very Low: Alternate between the high and low octaves.

104. Voice Chanting a Word: Chant any inspiring word and explore the microtonal possibilities between each note.

ENDINGS

105. Benediction (*Sanctus Dominus*): Improvise any slow melody and chant these Latin words of blessing.

106. Dedication (*Lokah Samasta Sukinho Bhavantu*): Improvise any melody and use it to chant these Tibetan words, which are a dedication of your practice to the benefit of all sentient beings. See "Vedic Prayer for Peace and Well-Being" in chapter 7, page 129. Listen to audio track 23.

107. Chant for Peace (*Om Shanti Shanti Shanti*): This Hindu prayer for peace is a lovely way to close your practice.

Chant this phrase using any simple melody. Listen to track 32: Chant for Peace *(Om Shanti Shanti Shanti)*.

108. Voice Playing with Silence: Rest in the sound of silence. Abide. Dwell.

Finale

All of what I love about singing is in these pages. This book is a poetic take on the power of the singing voice to make us feel freer and better. It is not a scientific tract. I want to give more people the chance to sing—to reclaim their birthright and explore the potential of resonance . . . and the transformation that follows.

Welcome to Planet Music.

Acknowledgments

From Silvia Nakkach

I have been writing this book all my life—on napkins, old notebooks, and outdated computers. The driving force for my assembling all these pieces of knowledge into a single book has been my students' continued request. Therefore, I want to thank them first for being my inspiration, my teachers, and my sonic family.

I owe my deepest appreciation to my life-long mentors, all four of whom I happened to meet in the same month and year: February 1982. They are the inner voices revealed throughout the teachings in this book: Ali Akbar Khan (Khansahib) who is the prana, the life force, that ignites my musical imagination; W. A. Mathieu (Allaudin) who trusted me from the beginning; Claudio Naranjo, the fascinating thinker and author, who opened doors for me for decades-to-come and awakened my consciousness to the mysticism of sound and life; and Pauline Oliveros, whom I "magically" met while walking down from a Zen mountain temple in Woodstock, New York, just when I was seeking guidance. Pauline's contemplative approach to sound shaped the spine of my own sound body—and continues to do so. My close encounters with each of these great teachers felt like being struck by lightning four times within a few days. These great teachers are always like new music in my life. How lucky could I be?

I have profound gratitude for many more master artists and colleagues who became my dear friends and have blessed my music and this book: Mayumi Oda, John Beaulieu, Thea Beaulieu, Janis Phelps, Swami Sitaramananda, Ritwik Sanyal, David Darling, Kit Walker, Meredith Monk, Kate and Andrew Geller, Mitchell Gaynor, Clive Robbins, Joanne Loewy, Myan Baker, Laura Condominas, Susana Bustos, Pat Cook, Ralph Metzner, and Don Campbell. Thank you for your unconditional support and inspiration.

I am wholeheartedly grateful to the gurus of my body: Barbara Voinar, the most mindful yoga teacher ever, and Sharon Pelle, a true bodhisattva of bodywork, who listened deeply when my body cried. Without them, I wouldn't have been able to sit straight for so many hours in front of my computer as I was writing.

I am deeply grateful to those who helped me to create this book and the accompanying audio teachings: Christopher Eickmann (an exquisite composer and sound engineer); Voice Divina, my vocal ensemble composed of Francine Lancaster, Jane Erwin Hammet, Hilary Reed, and Aletha McGee; and the hypnotic voices of Lama Pema Tenzin and Tsewong Sitar Rinpoche. Special thanks go to my life collaborators: Alba Lirio of Vox Mundi Rio and Michael Knapp, who drops pearls with each cello note.

I want to thank my agent Barbara Moulton for her presence at all times, and I must say that the team at Sounds True made the creation of this book into a lovely journey. In particular, I would like to acknowledge Jennifer Brown's nurturing guidance, and I'd like to thank my gentle and precise editors: Laurel Kallenbach, Haven Iverson, and the "team." My only wish is to work with them forever!

Finally, I am most indebted to my mind teachers who blessed me with the discovery that the voice is energy: Chagdud

Tulku Rinpoche, Chögyal Namkhai Norbu Rinpoche, Anam
Thubten Rinpoche, and Tenzin Wangyal Rinpoche. They protect my mind through the practice of Guru Yoga. To you, and
for the re-enchanting of all sentient beings, I send the longest
ahhhhhhhhhhhhhhhhhhhhhhhhhhhhhhhhh.

FROM VALERIE CARPENTER

I extend my deep gratitude to Barbara Moulton, literary agent
extraordinaire, whose belief and encouragement shepherded
this book from start to finish; to Hank Wesselman and his
knack for opening doors; to our editors Laurel Kallenbach
and Haven Iverson, and to all the wonderful folks at Sounds
True. Many thanks to Samira Michelson for her invaluable
research contributions and unconditional support, and to
my husband and champion Rob Carpenter, whose support
made this book possible. I am deeply indebted to the friends
and colleagues whose loving kindness was an endless blessing: Lynn Kirkham, Carol Hulley, Hilary Reed, Nicole Becker
(whose inspired yoga classes kept my body fit for longs days
at the computer), Julia Carpenter, and Heidi Irgens. And a
very special "thank you" must go to my exceptional high-
school English teacher, Lydia Esslinger, who always believed
that, one day, I would write a book.

Notes

CHAPTER 2: MUSIC AS MEDICINE

1. Alfred A. Tomatis, *The Conscious Ear* (New York: Station Hill Press, Inc., 1991), 217.
2. Mitchell L. Gaynor, *The Healing Power of Sound: Recovery from Life-Threatening Illnesses Using Sound, Voice, and Music* (Boston: Shambhala Publications, Inc., 2002), 26.
3. Michael Roizen and Mehmet Oz, "Sing to your health; crooning is good for you," *The Register Guard*, April 18, 2011.
4. Michael Meade, *The Great Dance: Finding One's Way in Troubled Times* (Mosaic Multicultural Foundation 7472760, 2007), compact disc.
5. Stephen S. Mehler, *From Light into Darkness* (Illinois: Adventures Press, 2005), 55.
6. Helen Gatling-Austin, "The Healing Power of Sound: An Interview with Tenzin Wangyal Rinpoche," *The Voice of Clear Light, News and Inspiration from Ligmincha Institute.* Vol. IV, No. 4, April 5, 2004.
7. Mingtong Gu, *Sound Healing Technologies.* DVD, Chi Center, 2010. 35.
8. "How Singing Improves Your Health (Even if Other People Shouldn't Hear You Singing)," *SixWise.com: Epiphanies for Your Empowerment,* May 7, 2011.

9. Gaynor, *The Healing Power of Sound*, 80–82.
10. Ibid., 52.
11. Ibid., 160–161.
12. Ibid., 160–163.
13. John Beaulieu, *Human Tuning: Sound Healing with Tuning Forks* (High Falls, NY: BioSonic Enterprises, Ltd., 2010), 56.
14. Ruth SoRelle, "Cardiovascular News: Nobel Prize Awarded to Scientists for Nitric Oxide Discoveries," *Circulation* 1998; 98:2365-2366, doi:10.1161/01.CIR.98.22.2365, accessed September 2011.
15. Beaulieu, *Human Tuning*, 55–56.
16. M. Maniscalco, et al. "Humming-induced Release of Nasal Nitric Oxide for Assessment of Sinus Obstruction in Allergic Rhinitis: Pilot Study." *European Journal of Clinical Investigation*, 34.8 (2004), 555-560.
17. Don Campbell, *The Mozart Effect: Tapping the Power of Music to Heal the Body, Strengthen the Mind, and Unlock the Creative Spirit* (New York: Harper Collins), 103.
18. Pierre Sollier, *Listening for Wellness: An Introduction to the Tomatis Method* (China: Everbest Printing Co. Ltd., 2005), 64.
19. Ibid., 75.
20. Daniel J. Levitin, *The World in Six Songs: How the Musical Brain Created Human Nature* (New York: Dutton, 2008), 39.
21. "Science—How iLs Works," Integrated Listening Systems, Inc., accessed January 20, 2012, integratedlistening.com/research-science.
22. William J. Cromie, "Music on the brain: Researchers explore the biology of music," *Harvard University Gazette*, accessed January 20, 2012, news.harvard.edu/gazette/2001/03.22/04-music.html.
23. Ibid.
24. Nancy Helm-Estabrooks, Marjorie Nicholas, Alisa R. Morgan, *Melodic Intonation Therapy* (Austin, TX: Pro-Ed., Inc., 1989).
25. Joanne V. Loewy, *Caring for the Caregiver: The Use of Music and Music Therapy in Grief and Trauma*, edited by Joanne

V. Loewy and Andrea Frisch Hara (Silver Spring, MD: The American Music Therapy Association Inc., 2007), 162.

26. Ibid.
27. Ibid., 118–124.
28. Sky Films, Inc., "The Singing Revolution," accessed September 30, 2011, http://www.singingrevolution.com/cgi-local/content.cgi?pg=1
29. Ibid.
30. Nicole Becker, Owner, Ojas Yoga Center, El Cerrito, CA, interview with Valerie Carpenter, June 23, 2011.

CHAPTER 3: PERMISSION TO SING

1. W.A. Mathieu, *The Musical Life: Reflections on What It Is and How to Live It* (Boston: Shambhala Publications, Inc., 1994), 59.
2. Hazrat Inayat Khan, *The Mysticism of Sound and Music* (Boston: Shambhala Publications, Inc., 1991) 172.
3. Chögyal Namkhai Norbu, *The Dzogchen Ritual Practices* (Paris: Kailash Editions, 1991).

CHAPTER 4: OUR MYSTICAL INSTRUMENT

1. Hilda Deighton and Gina Palermo, *Singing and the Etheric Tone: Gracia Ricardo's Approach to Singing, Based on her Work with Rudolf Steiner* (Hudson, NY: Anthroposophic Press, 1991), 15.
2. Ibid., 93.
3. Ibid., 16.
4. Ibid., 15.

CHAPTER 5: THE BODY OF THE VOICE

1. Joseph D. Brain, ScD, "Control of Breathing," *Merck Manual Online*, Merck Sharp & Dohme Corp, modified August 2006,

accessed September 30, 2011, merckmanuals.com/home/lung_
and_airway_disorders/biology_of_the_lungs_and_airways/
control_of_breathing.html

2. Hilda Deighton and Gina Palermo, *Singing and the Etheric Tone,* 17.

CHAPTER 6: IN THE BEGINNING, THERE WAS NOTHING BUT NADA

1. *The Essential Rumi,* trans. Coleman Barks (New York: Harper Collins, 2004), 6.

2. Costantino Albini, "The Magic Sound," *The Mirror* (newspaper of the International Dzogchen Community of Chögyal Namkhai Norbu), Issue No. 37, 1996, 17.

3. Ritwik Sanyal and Richard Widdess, *Dhrupad: Tradition and Performance in Indian Music* (Surrey, UK: Ashgate Publishing Group, 2004), 153.

4. Osho, "Nadabrahma," in *The Buddha Disease: A Darshan Diary* (Poona, India: Rajneesh Foundation Limited, 1979), 578.

5. Lokesh Chandra, "Musical Deities in Buddhism," in *Song of the Spirit: The World of Sacred Music,* (New Delhi: Tibet House, 2000), 149.

6. Pauline Oliveros, *Deep Listening: A Composer's Sound Practice* (Kingston, NY: Deep Listening Publications, 2005).

7. Osho, "Nadabrahma," 578.

CHAPTER 7: THE YOGA OF THE VOICE

1. Victor Zuckerkandl, *Sound and Symbol: Music and the External World* (New York: Pantheon Books, 1956), 37.

2. Dane Rudhyar, *The Magic of Tone and the Art of Music* (Boston: Shambhala Publications, Inc., 1982), 23.

3. Helen Gatling-Austin, "The Healing Power of Sound: An Interview with Tenzin Wangyal Rinpoche," *Snow Lion*

Publications, December 29, 2003, www.snowlionpub.com/
pages/wangyalteaching2.html.

4. Tenzin Wangyal Rinpoche, *Tibetan Sound Healing* (Boulder,
   CO: Sounds True, Inc., 2006), 19–82.
5. Helen Gatling-Austin, "The Healing Power of Sound: An
   Interview with Tenzin Wangyal Rinpoche."
6. W. A. Mathieu, *Harmonic Experience: Tonal Harmony from
   Its Natural Origins to Its Modern Expression* (Rochester, VT:
   Inner Traditions Intl, Ltd., 1997).
7. Pandit Usharbudh Arya, *Mantra and Meditation*
   (Pennsylvania: Himalayan Publishers, 1981), 182.
8. Lisa Clayton, "An Interview with Joan Chittister," *Sacred
   Journey, the Journal of Fellowship in Prayer,* Winter 2010.
9. Don Campbell's quote is from the foreword to: Robert Gass
   and Kathleen Brehony, *Chanting: Discovering Spirit in Sound*
   (New York: Broadway Books, 1999), ix.
10. George Harrison, "My Sweet Lord," from the album *All
    Things Must Pass,* Apple Records, 1970.

CHAPTER 8: MUSIC À LA MODE

1. Daniel J. Levitin, *This is Your Brain on Music: The Science of
   a Human Obsession* (New York: Dutton, 2006), 115–116.
2. Ibid., 116.
3. W. A. Mathieu, *The Listening Book: Discovering Your Own
   Music* (Boston: Shambhala Publications, Inc., 1991), 168.
4. Dane Rudhyar, *The Magic of Tone and the Art of Music*
   (Boston: Shambhala Publications, Inc., 1982), 84–85.
5. Olivier Messiaen, *The Technique of My Musical Language*
   (Paris: Leduc, 1944), 52.
6. Ibid.
7. Robin MacOnie, *Stockhausen on Music: Lectures and
   Interviews* (London: Marion Boyars, 2000).
8. Robert Sherlaw Johnson, *Messiaen* (Berkeley, CA: University
   of California Press, 1989), 32.

9. Ravi Shankar, "On Appreciation of Indian Classical Music," The Ravi Shankar Foundation, 2011, accessed July 15, 2011, www.ravishankar.org/indian_music.html.

10. Ali Akhar College of Music website, accessed June 29, 2011, aacm.org/school_faculty_aak.html.

11. Deepak S. Raja, *Hindustani Music: A Tradition in Transition* (New Delhi: D.K. Printworld, 2005).

12. Ibid.

13. Rhagava R. Menon, "The Predicament of Raga Music," in *Dhvani: Nature and Culture of Sound,* ed. S. C. Malik (New Delhi: Indira Gandhi National Center for the Arts, 1999), 55–56.

CHAPTER 9: DESIGNING YOUR PRACTICE

1. Chögyam Trungpa Rinpoche, *Dharma Art* (Boston: Shambhala Publications, Inc., 1996), 1–2.

Glossary

A

abrir caminhos: Portuguese, meaning "to open the ways."

adaptogen: A term used by herbalists to refer to a natural substance that has a normalizing effect on bodily processes.

adbhuta: One of the ten rasas. It evokes wonder, surprise, and the fantastic.

adrenaline: A hormone, secreted in response to stress, that raises heart and pulse rates, blood pressure, and blood levels of glucose and lipids.

adrsta-phala: Sanskrit, meaning "unseen fruit." It refers to spiritual benefit.

Aeolian mode: A musical mode, identified as the natural minor scale.

alap: The opening section of a typical North Indian classical-music performance. It is unmetered, improvised, and accompanied only with a drone.

anahad nada: Sanskrit, meaning "unlimited sound," or music of the highest sphere.

anahata nada: Sanskrit, meaning "the sound that is not made from two things striking together." It refers to the "unstruck sound" or primordial sound of the universe. It is the sound that is not heard except in the heart and in ecstatic consciousness. The heart center is also called "anahata."

aperiodicity: (also non-periodicity) In music, the lack of recurrence or repetition at regular intervals. The opposite of periodicity or steady pulse.

arpeggio: The notes of a chord played in succession, either ascending or descending.

articulation: The act of vocal expression, utterance, or enunciation.

asana: Sanskrit, meaning "to be present." Used in yoga to refer to a posture or pose.

ash: The name given to the sound of the **tamboura,** evoking the echoes of the Breath of God.

ashé: From the Yoruba *asé,* the ultimate source of everything.

autonomic nervous system: The part of the nervous system responsible for control of the bodily functions not consciously directed, such as breathing, the heartbeat, and digestive processes.

ayurveda: The traditional system of Hindu medicine, which uses diet, herbs, oils, massage, and yogic practices.

B

bhakti: One of the ten rasas. It evokes devotion.

bhakti yoga: The yogic path of pure spiritual devotion to the divine.

bija: Sanskrit, meaning "seed." A mantric syllable with which deities and other divine objects are summoned.

Brahma: In Hinduism, the Creator God.

C

chakra: From Sanskrit, meaning "wheel." It refers to the centers of spiritual energy in the human body.

chi: Chinese (also **qi**); the circulating life energy inherent in all living things.

cochlea: The spiral cavity of the inner ear containing the organ of Corti, which produces nerve impulses in response to sound vibrations.

consonant: In music, an aesthetically pleasing sensation or perception associated with the interval of the octave, the perfect fourth and fifth, the major and minor third and sixth, and chords based on these intervals.

cortex: The outer layer of the cerebrum (the cerebral cortex), composed of folded gray matter, that plays an important role in consciousness.

cortisol: A hormone released by the adrenal gland in response to stress.

countermelody: A secondary melody sounded simultaneously with the principal one.

D

degree: In music, each of the seven notes of the diatonic scale (*do re mi*, etc.).

dharana: Sanskrit term meaning "unbending concentration of the mind." Single-pointed attention.

dhrupad: Said to be the oldest vocal tradition in Hindustani classical music.

dissonant: In music, a sensation commonly associated with all intervals of the second and seventh, all diminished and augmented intervals, and all chords based on these intervals.

Dorian mode: A musical mode, using a minor scale.

drone: A continuous tone that establishes a harmonic center and may involve many partial harmonies and sonorities.

Dzogchen: According to Tibetan Buddhism and Bön, the natural, primordial state or natural condition of the mind, and a body of teachings and meditation practices aimed at realizing that condition.

E

embouchure: In music, the manner in which one's lips and tongue are applied to the mouthpiece of an instrument or shaped to produce a vocal tone.

etheric body: A concept promoted by Rudolf Steiner to refer to the subtle life-force body, which sustains the life of the physical body, and serves as the repository for the life-force or **prana**.

etheric tone: A concept promoted by Rudolf Steiner to refer to a quality of the singing tone that is influenced by and based upon spiritual scientific principles and views of anthroposophy.

G

ghandharva: Celestial being in Hinduism known for its superb musical skills.

guru yoga: Devotional contemplative practices associated with Tibetan Buddhism in which a student forms an identification with the guru or teacher by visualizing him or herself as of the same fundamental nature, thereby transmitting the virtuous qualities of a Buddha to the adept.

H

ha: Hawaiian, meaning "breath."

harmonium: A free-standing keyboard instrument similar to a reed organ. Sound is produced by air being blown through sets of free reeds, resulting in a sound similar to that of an accordion.

hasta prayaogas: Movements of the hands and arms as described by the Sama Vedas, ancient Hindu texts.

hasya: One of the ten rasas. It evokes laughter, celebration, and joy.

I

icaro: Medicine song used by shamans and healers (curanderos) in the Peruvian Amazon.

interval: In music, a combination of two notes or the distance between their pitches.

Ionian mode: A musical mode, identical to the modern major scale.

J

japa: Sanskrit; a spiritual discipline involving the meditative repetition of a mantra or name of divine power.

K

karuna: One of the ten rasas. It evokes pathos, longing, and loss.

ki: Japanese/Korean; the circulating life energy inherent in all living things.

kirtan (or kirtana): Sanskrit meaning "to repeat." Call-and-response chanting performed in India's devotional traditions.

koan: In Zen Buddhism, a story, question, or statement that cannot be understood by rational thinking.

komal: Sanskrit, meaning "soft." Used in music to refer to flatted notes.

kundalini: In Hinduism, energy that lies dormant at the base of the spine until it is activated, as by the practice of yoga, and channeled upward through the chakras in the process of spiritual perfection.

L

Locrian mode: A musical mode with a bit of creative dissonance.

lung: Tibetan, meaning "wind" or "breath."

Lydian mode: A musical mode with an unpredictable flavor.

M

mandala: Sanskrit, meaning "circle." A form used in Hindu and Buddhist sacred art as a tool to teach peace and unity. It can also be conceived as a "home" for the sacred.

mantra: An empowered word or phrase that is chanted repetitively as a tool for spiritual transformation in order to empty the mind and attain oneness with cosmic consciousness.

maqam: In Arabic music, a set of notes with traditions that define relationships between them, their habitual patterns, and their melodic development.

medicine melody: A short and simple tonal configuration of notes that has the power to heal body, mind, and emotions. These melodies are "received" by a practitioner in an ecstatic state of mind that reflects a sacred unity with nature and the spirit world.

meend: In Hindustani music, the practice of gliding from one note to another, in microtonal increments.

Melodic Intonation Therapy (MIT): A therapeutic process that uses singing to stimulate activity in the right hemisphere of the brain in order to assist in speech production in patients with communication disorders caused by brain damage.

melodic phrase: A succession of notes forming a distinctive sequence.

meter: In music, the measurement of the number of **pulses** between more or less regularly recurring accents.

Mixolydian mode: A musical mode with a folksy flavor.

modal music: Music related to one of the modes where the melodic structure moves around a tone center.

mode: In music, this refers to a type of scale or a particular tonal arrangement.

mudra: From Sanskrit, meaning "seal" or "symbol." Refers to a hand gesture used in yoga or ritual dance that conveys symbolic meaning and energetic virtue.

N

nada: Sanskrit, meaning "sound" or "vibration."

Nada Brahma: Sanskrit, combining "sound" with Brahma, the Creator God; implying both the "Sound of God" and that "Sound is God."

nada yoga: The yoga of sound and vibration.

neocortex: A part of the cerebral cortex concerned with sight and hearing in mammals, regarded as the most recently evolved part of the cortex.

neuroplasticity: A concept that refers to the brain's ability to essentially rewire itself in response to experience.

nitric oxide: A molecule, fundamental to all life, that is produced inside vascular, nerve, and immune cells and is released into surrounding tissues as a gas.

non-periodicity: (also **aperiodicity**) In music, the lack of recurrence or repetition at regular intervals.

O

ossicle: A small bone, especially one of the three bones of the middle ear.

ostinato: A motif or pattern that is persistently repeated in the same musical voice.

overtone: A musical tone that is a part of the harmonic series above a fundamental note and may be heard with it.

P

parasympathetic nervous system: A part of the nervous system that serves to slow the heart rate, increase intestinal and glandular activity, and relax the sphincter muscles.

periodicity: In music, recurrence or repetition at regular intervals.

phonation: The sound made by the vibration of vocal folds modified by the resonance of the vocal tract.

phoneme: A perceptually distinct unit of sound.

Phrygian mode: A musical mode, typically heard in flamenco music.

piccolo: Italian, meaning "small."

point of entry: Any practice, technique, or inspiration leading into a musical or vocal improvisation.

polyphony: Music with two or more independent melodic parts sounded together.

portamento: In music, a smooth, uninterrupted glide from one note to another.

prana: Sanskrit, meaning "vital life;" the life force or vital energy that permeates the body.

pranayama: Sanskrit, meaning "restraint of the prana or breath."

pulse: In music, the equal division of beats.

R

raagini box: An electronic device that simulates the sound of a tamboura and is used as a drone accompaniment.

raga: A tonal arrangement of notes governed by specific rules for ascending and descending the scale.

rasa: Sanskrit meaning "essence," "taste," "flavor," "sap," or "juice." That which gives taste to the mind. The concept of aesthetic flavor, or the essential mood or sentiment conveyed by any work of art.

rasika: A person who has some knowledge of and is able to appreciate the aesthetic quality (rasa) of music or any work of art.

relaxation response: A physical state of deep rest that alters the physical and emotional responses to stress.

resonance: A phenomenon that occurs when the vibratory rate of a thing is changed in response to the vibration of an external force or object.

S

sadja: Sanskrit; the full name of Sa, the first note or tonic of a classical Indian scale, derived from *sad* (six) and *aja* (creator of).

samaswara: Sanskrit; a system of musical notation dating from the late Vedic period (1000 BC), from which the **sargam** originates.

Saraswati: Hindu goddess of knowledge, music, and the arts. Her name means "she who flows and endows beauty and wisdom to all things that sound."

sargam: Sanskrit; a system of musical notation in Indian classical music, derived from the names of the first four notes: Sa, Re, Ga, Ma.

seed syllable: Ancient sound formulas charged with spiritual information.

shabda: Sanskrit, meaning "sound," "speech," or "utterance" in the sense of linguistic performance.

shabda yoga: Yoga of the inspired word, in the realm of language and meaning, specifically the practice of chanting seed syllables and mantras.

shaddra: Sanskrit, meaning unconditional "reverence" of a spiritual nature.

shanti: One of the ten rasas. It evokes inner peace.

shringar: One of the ten rasas. It evokes eroticism, passion, and divine sensuality.

sruti: Sanskrit, meaning "that which can be revealed." In music, a sruti is one of the twenty-two microtones that exists between the principle notes or **swaras.**

sruti box: A small wooden instrument that traditionally works with bellows and is used as a drone accompaniment.

shuddha: Sanskrit, meaning "pure." Used in music to refer to natural notes (that are neither flatted nor sharped).

soham: Sanskrit, meaning "I am that." A powerful mantra that denotes the oneness of every living being by means of breath as life force.

solfeggio: Italian; a technique used in Western music for the teaching of sight singing.

sopro: Portuguese, meaning "blow, blowing, breath."

sulle labbra: Italian, meaning "on the lips."

sutra: In Hindu and Buddhist traditions, a scriptural narrative derived from ancient teachings and sacred texts.

swara: Sanskrit; the notes of the sargam, the Indian scale.

sympathetic nervous system: A part of the nervous system that serves to accelerate the heart rate, constrict blood vessels, and raise blood pressure.

T

Taizé: An ecumenical monastic order in France, known for the beauty of their meditative singing.

tamboura: A large, four-stringed lute used in Indian music as a drone accompaniment.

tessitura: Italian; the prevailing range of a vocal or instrumental part within which most of the tones lie.

That: Sanskrit, meaning "framework." The ten thats refer to the organization of ragas into a system of scales (each consisting of seven different notes or swaras) in North Indian classical music.

timbre: The combination of qualities of a sound that distinguishes it from other sounds of the same pitch and volume.

tivra: Sanskrit, meaning "sharp"; used in music to refer to notes that are sharp.

tonal music (also tonality): A system of music in which specific hierarchical pitch relationships are based on a key "center," or tonic.

tonic: In music, the first note of the diatonic scale and the tonal center of the final resolution tone.

tyag: One of the ten rasas. It evokes renunciation and detachment.

V

vagus nerve: The tenth (and longest) of the cranial nerves that passes through the neck and thorax into the abdomen, and supplies sensation to part of the ear, the tongue, the larynx, and the pharynx; motor impulses to the vocal cords; and motor and secretory impulses to the abdominal and thoracic viscera.

vairagya: Sanskrit term that roughly translates as dispassion, detachment, or renunciation.

Veda: Any of the oldest and most authoritative Hindu sacred texts.

Vedic: Of or relating to the Vedas, the oldest and most authoritative Hindu sacred texts.

vestibular system: The system of fluid-filled canals in the inner ear that assists in balance, coordination, and orientation.

vibrato: A tremulous or pulsating effect produced in an instrumental or vocal tone by minute and rapid variations in pitch.

vira: One of the ten rasas. It evokes heroism, courage, and valor.

vocable: A word considered only as a sequence of sounds rather than a unit of meaning.

vocal meditation: Signature practice of the Yoga of the Voice that involves singing with a drone, moving slowly from one note to the next.

Resources

Creative Scores: Recording, arranging, and production studio, founded
by composer Christopher Eickmann. (creativescores.com)

Gaynor Integrative Oncology: Founded by Dr. Mitchell Gaynor
who is at the forefront in new strategies for both the treatment
and prevention of cancer, including sound healing and
nutrition. Dr. Gaynor tailors treatments to individual patient
needs. (gaynoroncology.com)

The Chi Center, LLC: Founded by Master Mingtong Gu, its
mission is to facilitate the integration of mind, body, and spirit
through the knowledge, love, and energy of the ancient art and
new science of qigong. (chicenter.com)

RECOMMENDED READING

In addition to the following books and articles, further reading can
be found on the Vox Mundi website under Recommended Reading:
voxmundiproject.com.

Ball, Philip. *The Music Instinct: How Music Works and Why We
Can't Do Without It*. London: Oxford University Press, 2010.

Beaulieu, John. *Human Tuning: Sound Healing with Tuning Forks*.
High Falls, NY: BioSonic Enterprises, Ltd., 2010.

Boyce-Tillman, June. *Constructing Musical Healing: The Wounds
that Sing*. London: Jessica Kingsley, 2000.

Campbell, Don and Alex Doman. *Healing at the Speed of Sound:
How What We Hear Transforms Our Brains and Our Lives*.
New York: Hudson Street Press, 2011.

Daniélou, Alain. *Music and the Power of Sound*. Rochester, VT:
Inner Traditions, 1943.

———. *Sacred Music: Its Origins, Powers and Future*. Varanasi,
India: Indica Books, 2003.

Dileo C. and J. V. Loewy, eds. *Music Therapy at the End of Life*.
Cherry Hill, NJ: Jeffrey Books, 2005.

Eliade, Mircea. *Yoga, Immortality and Freedom*. Princeton, NJ:
Princeton Univerity Press, Bollingen Series, 1954, 1969.

Gaynor, Mitchell L. *The Healing Power of Sound: Recovery from Life-Threatening Illnesses Using Sound, Voice, and Music.* Boston: Shambala, 2002.

Hanser, Suzanne B. *The New Music Therapy Handbook.* Boston: Berklee Music Press, 1999.

Inayat Khan, Hazrat. *The Mysticism of Sound and Music.* Boston: Shambhala Publications, Ltd., 1996.

Keyes, Laurel Elizabeth. *Toning: The Creative Power of the Voice.* Marina del Ray, CA: DeVorss & Co., 1973.

Levitin, Daniel J. *The World in Six Songs: How the Musical Brain Created Human Nature.* New York: Dutton, 2008.

———. *This is Your Brain on Music: The Science of a Human Obsession.* New York: Dutton, 2006.

MacOnie, Robin. *Stockhausen on Music: Lectures and Interviews.* London: Marion Boyars, 2000.

Mathieu, W. A. *Harmonic Experience.* Rochester, VT: Inner Traditions, 1997.

———. *The Listening Book: Discovering Your Own Music.* Boston: Shambhala Publications, Inc., 1991.

———. *The Musical Life: Reflections on What It Is and How to Live It.* Boston: Shambhala Publications, Ltd., 1994.

Moffitt Cook, Pat. *Shaman, Jhankri, & Nele: Sound Healers of Indigenous Cultures.* Washington: Open Ear Press, 1997, 2004.

Nakkach, Silvia. *Music in Human Adaptation.* Dr. Daniel J. Schneck and Judith K. Schneck, eds. Blacksburg, VA: Polytechnic Institute and State University, 1997.

Namkhai Norbu, Chögyal. *Dzogchen Teachings.* Ithaca, NY: Snow Lion, 2006.

———. *Dzogchen, The Self-Perfected State.* Ithaca, NY: Snow Lion, 2003.

———. *The Crystal and the Way of Light.* Ithaca, NY: Snow Lion, 1999.

———. *The Mirror: Advice on the Presence of Awareness.* Barrytown, NY: Barrytown Limited, 1996.

Oliveros, Pauline. *Deep Listening: A Composer's Sound Practice.* Kingston, NY: Deep Listening Publications, 2005.

Regunathan, Sudhamahi, ed. *Song of the Spirit: The World of Sacred Music.* New Delhi: Tibet House, 2000.

Reid, Cornelius L. *Voice: Psyche and Soma.* New York: Joseph Patelson Music House, 1975.

Rouget, Gilbert. *Music and Trance.* Chicago and London: Chicago Press, 1985.

Ruckert, George and Ali Akbar Khan, eds. *The Classical Music of North India.* Saint Louis, MO: MMB Music, Inc., 1991.

Rudhyar, Dane. *The Magic of Tone and the Art of Music.* Boulder, CO: Shambhala Publications, Inc., 1982.

Sacks, Oliver. *Musicophilia: Tales of Music and the Brain.* New York: Knopf, 2007.

Schneck, Daniel J. and Judith K. Schneck, eds. *Music in Human Adaptation.* Blacksburg, VA: Virginia Tech Press, 1997.

Sing the Name. South Fallsburg, NY: Siddha Yoga publications, 1997.

Stockhausen, Karlheinz. *Towards a Cosmic Music.* Shaftesburg, Dorset: Elements Books Limited,1989.

Tomatis, Alfred A. *The Conscious Ear.* New York: Station Hill Press, Inc., 1991.

Trungpa, Chögyam. *Dharma Art.* Boston & London: Shambhala, 1996.

Vishnu-Devananda, Swami. *Meditation and Mantras.* New York: Om Lotus Publishing, 1978, 2000.

Wangyal, Tenzin. *Tibetan Sound Healing.* Boulder, CO: Sounds True, Inc., 2006.

Wolfsohn, Alfred and The Roy Hart Theatre, his theories, lectures and recordings, www.roy-hart.com, http://www.roy-hart.com/writingsaboutawe.htm

Recommended Listening: Listening for Change

Dedicate a day to what I call a "listening diet," devoting three hours to listening to music you've never heard before. Keep a notebook nearby where you can write the highlights of your auditory experience (how the music impacted your body, mind, mood, fantasy). Turn off your phone, and make sure you will not be interrupted. Relax with a nice cup of tea or just water. View this practice as a listening meditation. Create silent breaks in between, whenever you feel like it. The key is just to listen without comparing the music from one album to another.

The music on this list may change you as much as it has me. Use this discography to inspire you to compile your own musical biography with works by musicians who made you who you are today. I suggest starting with the following compositions, which I recommend both for seasoned and first-time listeners. Imagine we are listening together. . . . Viva la Musica!

Bach, Johann Sebastian. *Goldberg Variations.* 1741.
Beaulieu, John. *Calendula.* 1997.
Bethania, Maria. *Pirata.* 2007.
Cage, John. *In A Landscape.* 1995.
Darling, David with Ketil Bjørnstad. *Epigraphs.* 2000.
———. *Cello Blue.* 2001
Eno, Brian. *The Shutov Assembly.* 1992.
Figueras, Monserrat. *Ninna Nanna.* 2005.
Gismonti, Egberto. *Sol do Meio Dia.* 1978.
Güven, Rahmi Oruç and Tumata. *Ocean of Remembrance.* 1995.
Khan, Alam. *Shades of Sarode.* 2011, CD.
Khan, Ali Akbar. *Ustad Ali Akbar Khan Plays Alap: A Sarode Solo.* 1993, 2 CD set.
Ligeti, György. "Lux Aeterna for 16 solo voices." 1966.
Mahler, Gustav. Adagio of Symphony #4. 1899–1901.
———. Adagios of all 10 symphonies.
Messiaen, Olivier. *Oiseaux Exotiques.* 1956.
———. *Quartet for the End of Time.* 1940.
Monk, Meredith. *The Book of Days.* 1988.
Nakkach, Silvia. *Ah: The Healing Voice.* 1998.
———. *Aya: Spirit Voices.* 2008.
———. *Invocation.* 2003.

———. *Medicine Melodies.* 2012.

———. *Musical Massage: Inside.* 2000.

———. *Unwind.* 2001.

Oliveros, Pauline with Stuart Dempster. *Panaiotis: Deep Listening.* 1989.

Pärt, Arvo. *Spiegel im Spiegel.* 1978.

Sanyal, Ritwik. Dhrupad. *Raga Ahir Bhairav.* 2007.

Savall, Jordi. *Les Voix Humaines.* 1998.

Scelsi, Giacinto. *Elegia per Ty.* 1989.

Stockhausen, Karlheinz. "Stimmung." 1977.

Veloso, Caetano. *Bossa de Caetano.* 2000, CD.

FILMS

Melancholia, directed by Lars von Trier (Denmark: Nordisk Film, 2011).

Of Gods and Men, directed by Xavier Beauvois (Armada Films, 2010).

Pina, directed by Wim Wenders (Berlin: Neue Road Movies, 2011).

Play Like a Lion: The Legacy of Maestro Ali Akbar Khan, directed by Joshua Dylan Mellars (Abuela Luna Pictures, 2011).

The King's Speech, directed by Tom Hopper. (The Weinstein Co. and Anchor Bay Entertainment, 2011).

The Music Instinct: Science and Song, directed by Elena Mannes (New York: PBS, 2009).

The Singing Revolution, directed by James Tusty and Maureen Castle Tusty (New York: Docurama Films, 2008).

Soundtrack for a Revolution, directed by Bill Guttentag and Dan Sturman (Louverture Films, 2009).

INSTRUMENTS

Sruti box: Ali Akbar College of Music, aacm.org/shop/
Tuning forks: BioSonics Enterprises, biosonics.com

HERBS FOR THE VOICE

Botanical tonics formulated by Donald Yance can be found through
Natura Health Products: naturahealthproducts.com

About Silvia Nakkach

An internationally known pioneer in the field of sound and transformation of consciousness, Silvia Nakkach, MA, MMT, has cultivated a voice that transports listeners into the heart of devotion. Her vocal work ranges from traditional chants to contemporary vocal improvisations. She is also an award-winning composer, former music psychotherapist, teacher, and recording artist.

Nakkach is the founding director of Vox Mundi School of the Voice, an international project devoted to teaching and preserving sacred-music traditions. Vox Mundi students study the integrative use of sound and chant to transform consciousness, to support healing, and to revitalize singing as spiritual practice. Vox Mundi has schools in the San Francisco Bay Area, Brazil, and Argentina.

Nakkach is on the faculty of the California Institute of Integral Studies in San Francisco, where she created the Sound, Voice, Music Healing Certificate and also designed the academic master's degree in integrative health with a focus on sound healing. She travels worldwide to lead trainings in the Yoga of the Voice, her signature program.

Nakkach's interest in indigenous music cosmology and spirituality has led her to collaborate with renowned Indian healers and South American shamans. In addition, she has studied Hindustani music with the late maestro Ali Akbar Khan, and Dhrupad singing with Dr. Ritwik Sanyal in Benares, India, where she travels annually with her students.

Nakkach, who holds degrees in music composition, psychology, music therapy, and music education, has written an opera (*Amazonia Insight*), released nine albums, and written many scholarly articles on the healing power of music. Her album, *Ah: The Healing Voice*, is played in hospitals and health-care centers to create a healing atmosphere before and after surgery. She has contributed to an extensive body of therapeutic vocal techniques that have become landmarks in the fields of sound healing and music therapy training.

For more information about Nakkach's research and teaching, visit voxmundiproject.com.

About Valerie Carpenter

Valerie Carpenter, MFA, is a Sound Healing practitioner in the San Francisco Bay Area, with certifications from the California Institute of Integral Studies, the Kairos Institute of Sound Healing, Integrated Listening Systems, and the Vox Mundi School of the Voice.

Carpenter has also enjoyed a distinguished career as a professional writer and actress with advanced degrees from Stanford University and NYU School of the Arts. Drawing on a vast array of experience as a performing artist, workshop facilitator, and intrepid explorer of the invisible realms, she offers a multi-modal sound-healing approach that embraces the shamanic healing arts. She has developed effective protocols for stress relief, grounding and centering, spiritual emergence, and trauma recovery, and works with individuals, couples, and groups.

Carpenter is the cofounder of the Bay Area Sound Healing Alliance (baysha.org), and the founding director of The Vestibule Center for Sound Healing, a community resource for healing, learning, expression, and personal growth. For more information, visit thevestibule.net.

About Sounds True

Sounds True is a multimedia publisher whose mission is to inspire and support personal transformation and spiritual awakening. Founded in 1985 and located in Boulder, Colorado, we work with many of the leading spiritual teachers, thinkers, healers, and visionary artists of our time. We strive with every title to preserve the essential "living wisdom" of the author or artist. It is our goal to create products that not only provide information to a reader or listener, but that also embody the quality of a wisdom transmission.

For those seeking genuine transformation, Sounds True is your trusted partner. At SoundsTrue.com you will find a wealth of free resources to support your journey, including exclusive weekly audio interviews, free downloads, interactive learning tools, and other special savings on all our titles.

To listen to a podcast interview with Sounds True publisher Tami Simon and author Silvia Nakkach, please visit SoundsTrue.com/bonus/FreeYourVoice.

SOUNDS True
many voices, one journey

Notes